THE WALT DISNEY WORLD GUIDE BOOK 2023

The Newest & Best Pro Tips for First Timers to Plan a Trip, Hacks to Skip the Line & Everything You Need to Know to Outsmart Disney World in 2023

Primeveler Publishing

TABLE OF CONTENTS

INTRODUCTION

In the past twenty years, people's travel habits have changed drastically. Most families are looking for authentic experiences that suit their needs and budgets rather than being misled by carefully marketed mega-resorts; with the average family size shrinking and people's disposable income increasing, they want to spend money on those specific things they enjoy most – not just on expensive food, fancy shops, and attractions.

Wherever we go, we always look for the best experience, quality, and price; what's more, we all have different expectations to choose from, and most importantly, we would like our vacation to be relaxing and hassle-free. Nowadays, having detailed travel advice at our fingertips is really important to us – it helps us plan and prepare for our travels, save time and money, and get necessary information in one place – all at our fingertips!

Walt Disney World may appear to be a park filled with the world's most popular cartoon characters at first glance, but over the years, it has become a world-renowned vacation destination for leisure and business travelers. It is one of the most popular tourist destinations in Florida and one of the most popular in the United States. From themed restaurants to limited-time thrilling attractions, you cannot always predict what will come next – is it a thrilling roller coaster or a relaxing boat ride? A long queue for popular rides or a short one for less popular ones?

This Walt Disney World Travel Guide has been written with this in mind: to provide you with an easy-to-read guide to the Walt Disney World Resort and its Vacation Planner, as well as with a detailed list of the best tips, advice, and recommendations – the good and the bad – to help you plan your next trip to Walt Disney World Resort!

This guide is for both that are newbies and for return visitors alike. It is not just a trip guide that talks about the historic Disney World; it is a guide that convinces you to visit Walt Disney World again and again. Different types of families have different needs, and there are several attractions to suit every taste! Thus, this guide will encompass all the information you need to plan your trip accordingly, from theme parks to accommodation, restaurants to children's activities, entertainment to shopping, transportation to landmarks, and everything in between.

This travel guide provides comprehensive information about the Walt Disney World resort and individual parks and tips, advice, and recommendations – the good and the bad – for planning your next trip to Walt Disney World Resort.

Overall, this guide will help you plan your trip accordingly and ensure you don't miss anything!

HISTORY OF WALT DISNEY WORLD

The Walt Disney World resort is a very large and complex tourist attraction that is based around the Mickey Mouse character, acting as an amusement park and a vacation resort. This 4,400-acre resort is located in Central Florida's Orange County on the east coast of Lake Buena Vista, just outside of Orlando, the greatest holiday destination on earth.

Disney World was first built in 1971 as a small family-orientated park located in Bay Lake, Florida, and it aimed to be a dream world for children. The park was made up of four major areas (Main Street, U.S.A., Tomorrowland, Fantasyland, and Adventureland), which were themed after the movies of Walt Disney - Snow White and Cinderella; this park was called Walt Disney World's Magic Kingdom!

The next phase in Disney World's development was in 1983 when EPCOT Center was completed based on Walt's idea that "a person can dream, and if he dreams with a big enough dream and works hard enough, he can make his dreams come true." This was the first Disney theme park that had been created under Walt Disney's original Theme Park Plan, aimed at blending the worlds of science-fiction with real life, as well as being a showcase for Disney's cutting-edge technology and imagination.

The third and most recent 'kingdom' was opened in 1989 as Animal Kingdom, a wildlife theme park showcasing the animals of Africa, Australia, and the Americas. This is home to the world's largest man-made lake, an endangered species animal sanctuary, and an extensive collection of Disney characters.

Over the years, many more attractions have been added to these parks, making them more exciting than ever! These included new rides, shows, restaurants, and hotels that were themed around popular Disney films such as Frozen, Pirates of the Caribbean, Jungle Cruise, and Beauty and the Beast.

Walt Disney World has been one of the world's most popular tourist destinations for over five decades. Just to put things into perspective, more than 52 million people visited Walt Disney World in 2016 alone - that's over 15 million more visitors each year compared to Las Vegas! However, this is still only a tiny percentage of the numbers that have visited Walt Disney World since it first opened its doors in 1971 - around 100 million visitors!

Since then, Disney World has grown and expanded a lot.

Theme Parks

The Walt Disney World Resort currently offers four theme parks that are each unique, exciting, and entertaining in their own way for guests of all ages to enjoy.

1. Magic Kingdom

This is the most popular Walt Disney World theme park. During the holidays and on weekends, this park is the most popular and attracts the greatest number of visitors. In fact, the Magic Kingdom attracts approximately 20 million visitors per year, roughly doubling the attendance of Disney's Animal Kingdom.

Magic Kingdom is the first park built in 1971 and located in Downtown Disney. The Magic Kingdom is the biggest and most popular theme park that is themed around classic fairy tales. On entering the park, you will find yourself surrounded by a magical castle, Cinderella's castle, that sits on top of a hill overlooking its fairytale surroundings. This castle is home to many of the characters from classic fairy tales, such as Mickey Mouse, Cinderella, Snow White, etc. Inside the park, there are many different lands for you to explore, with attractions, rides, and themes that are unique to each one of them.

Epcot Center is a theme park that was opened in 1982 on a 14-acre site near the Walt Disney World Resort and is based around the idea of 'managing, preserving and presenting the world's cultures.' This park is inspired by the development and advancement of society, the culture of countries around the world, and new ideas about technology, the environment, and modernization. The idea behind the park was that Walt had been on a visit to some of the most advanced cities in the world and had come up with the idea of a city that would combine science, optimism, and futurism. This is how EPCOT Center was born!

Epcot is one of the most iconic parks at Walt Disney World. With a theme centered on global travel and a massive centerpiece resembling a golf ball, Epcot attracts over 11 million visitors annually. Epcot is well-known for its cuisine and unique attractions.

It was the third of Walt Disney World's four theme parks to be constructed. It was inspired by the Golden Age of Hollywood and is devoted to the imagined worlds of film, television, music, and theater. Opened in 1989, Hollywood Studios entertains and amazes guests with memorable entertainment and attractions that are based on the history of this popular entertainment field.

The park is divided into four themed districts: the Sunset Boulevard district of Hollywood, the Music World district at The American Idol Experience, the Animation Courtyard, and the Echo Lake district.

4. Disney's Animal Kingdom

One of the first individuals to consider environmental and animal protection as a theme for a park was Walt Disney. The park was constructed on 580 acres (230 hectares) and opened on Earth Day, April 22, 1998. It is different from the other theme parks at Walt Disney World because it has both traditional rides and hundreds of species of real animals. In order to keep the animals safe, the park was built with special plans and features.

This enclosure is located on the western edge of the resort and is separated from the other theme parks and properties so that the animals are as unaffected by outside noises as possible. As a result, the previous nighttime show at the park lacked fireworks, which would have made the animals anxious.

Waterparks

There are two waterparks at Walt Disney World Resort.

1. Disney's Typhoon Lagoon

Image: Chad Sparkes from Kissimmee,Florida, United States

The water park is situated within the Walt Disney World Resort. It is one of two water parks that are open at the resort. It is the resort's second water park. The first one, Disney's River Country, closed in November 2001.

The park opened on June 1, 1989. It has one of the largest outdoor wave pools in the world, where you can even bodysurf. The park is based on the "Disney legend" of a typhoon that wrecked a tropical paradise that used to be perfect. The storm threw ships, fishing gear, and surfboards all over the place. Its main feature is "Miss Tilly," a shrimp boat stuck on a mountain called "Mount Mayday" that sends up a 50-foot (15 m) water geyser every half hour, right before the watch bells ring on it. It has a dark ride, "Splash Mountain," with two large waterfalls kids love riding.

Image: Jeff Kays

It is themed around a ski resort in the summer. All of the water areas are heated with the exception of the melting snow in the Cross Country Creek ice cave.

It opened on April 1, 1995, and about 2,091,000 people went to the park in 2016, making it the third-most-visited water park in the world, just behind its sister park, Typhoon Lagoon. Blizzard Beach is open all year except in the winter when it is closed for maintenance. During the time it was closed, its sister park, Typhoon Lagoon, entertained the guests.

Disney World is one of the largest Theme Parks in the world, with a huge variety of attractions, activities, entertainment, and events to enjoy. Aside from these, many hidden gems are worth checking out.

EVERYTHING NEEDED FOR A 2023 VISIT

Wanting to go to Walt Disney World is easy—planning your visit is challenging. Ensure you have everything you need for a successful trip.

Park Hours and Schedules

Hours at Disney World vary widely between parks, especially among theme parks.

1. The Magic Kingdom

The Magic Kingdom is the theme park with the most varied operating hours. The Magic Kingdom typically opens at 9:00 a.m., but the closing time can vary between 6:00 p.m. and 3:00 a.m., depending on the day and season. Usually, the park stays open an hour after the last scheduled show.

2. Epcot

EPCOT comprises two theme parks, World Showcase, and Future World. When it comes to Disney World Hours, EPCOT is the most consistent of the parks. Future World will open at 9:00 a.m. (8:00 in the morning during Extra Magic Hour) and begin closing at 7:00 p.m. On most days, the World Showcase will open at 11 a.m. and remain open until the park closes. EPCOT will close at 9 p.m. (during peak periods, 9:30 p.m.) and even later on a few major holidays. Some full-priced admissions tickets to EPCOT don't include the World Showcase and close before the World Showcase is closed.

3. Disney's Hollywood Studios

The majority of the time, Disney's Hollywood Studios opens with the other parks at 9:00 a.m., but closing time varies based on current events. Every evening, it is 7:00 p.m. During peak periods, it may be later than 10:00 p.m.

4. Disney's Animal Kingdom

It usually opens at 9:00 a.m., but as with the other parks, the closing time varies. It typically closes at 8:30 p.m. but can close as late as 10:00 p.m. During peak periods, it may be 10:00 p.m. or later.

5. Blizzard Beach

Disney's Blizzard Beach typically opens at 10:00 a.m., but closing time varies. It typically closes as late as 10:00 p.m. but may close as late as 11:30 p.m., depending on the day and season. It may be 10:00 p.m. or later during peak periods, but the beach will remain open until 11:30 p.m. On some days, the park can remain open until 12 or 1 a.m. On a select few holidays, Blizzard Beach will be closed permanently on those days instead of opening at 8:00 a.m.

6. Typhoon Lagoon

Disney's Typhoon Lagoon is typically open from 10 a.m. to 5 p.m., but the closing time can vary. It typically closes as late as 7:00 p.m. but may close as early as 6:30 p.m., depending on the day and season. It may be 8:30 p.m. or later during peak periods, but the beach will remain open until 8:30 p.m. On some days, the park can remain open until 9 or 10 p.m.

Monthly Breakdown

January

Overview:

The crowds from New Year's Eve have ended, but everyone is planning their trips for Presidents Day weekend and the week after. This means that there will be higher crowds than usual throughout the month.

Weather:

The temperature can range from the 50°F (10°C) to the 80°F (27°C) during daytime. At night, the high may reach the lower 60°F (16°C). Rain or snow is a possibility, but it doesn't happen often.

Least Crowded Days:

The middle of this month is still busy because everyone is planning to go then, but it's less crowded than other days in January. If you want to avoid crowds, the last two weeks of summer are also a good option, as the school has resumed and the weather is beginning to warm up.

Most Crowded Days:

The middle of the first week of January and the beginning of every week is always packed because everyone is planning to go then. New Year's Eve is another very crowded day, especially at Magic Kingdom. The rest of January can be packed as well, but weekends particularly on President's Day weekend and the weeks after, are a great time to go if you wish to avoid crowds.

Special Event: New Year's Eve (December 31st)

New Year's is a popular and crowded holiday that is widely observed at Walt Disney World. The Magic Kingdom and Epcot both display midnight fireworks. The Hollywood

Studios dance party continues until 1 a.m. The Tree of Life hosts a New Year's Eve countdown at Animal Kingdom.

Overview:

Possibly the least crowded month of the entire year, which is why it's one of the most popular for trips. The weather is still mild but gets slightly better as the months go by. Students have returned to school. Other major holidays like Valentine's Day and St. Patrick's Day can also have increased crowds.

Weather:

The weather is better, but not overly hot or cold. The temperature ranges between 60°F (16°C) and 80°F (27°C) during the daytime. At night, the high may reach the lower 60°F (16°C). Rain or snow is a possibility, but it doesn't happen often.

Least Crowded Days:

The week before and after Valentine's Day is generally the least crowded, although it has been known to get pretty crowded on St. Patrick's Day at Magic Kingdom. The week before and after Presidents Day is also a great time to go if you don't want a ton of people around.

Most Crowded Days:

The first two weeks of February have some really high crowds because everyone is planning their trips for that time period. The week after Presidents Day is also busy, although it's less busy than the rest of February.

Special Event: Epcot International Festival of The Arts (January 13 to February 20, 2023)

From music to specialty dishes and performances featuring drummers, mimes, and dancers, this event features a variety of live and animated entertainment. Bringing in celebrities, performers, and cooking demonstrations, the International Festival of The Arts is all about bringing people together to enjoy one another's cultures and enjoy the arts in a very special way.

Overview:

During this month, many people go to Florida during spring break, which can cause some heightened crowds. The weather is getting hotter and close to summer. The end of the month is also busy because the post-break season has started, but students have returned to school again.

Weather:

The weather during March is better than in February, but still neither hot nor cold. The temperature ranges from 50°F (10°C) to 80°F (27°C) during the daytime. The high may reach the mid 60°F (16°C) at night. March is known to have its occasional heatwaves, bringing the weather above 90°F (32°C). Rain or snow is a possibility, but it doesn't happen often.

Least Crowded Days:

The first Tuesday, Wednesday, and Thursday of the month are the least crowded. The beginning and the end of March can be really busy, but those days can be nice if you prefer to avoid crowds.

Most Crowded Days:

The last two weeks of March are always busy and crowded. Especially St.Patricks Day(March 17) and Spring Break.

Special Event: Epcot Flower and Garden Festival (March 1 through July 5, 2023)

The Flower and Garden Festival takes place at Epcot and features many gardening-themed events and activities, including hands-on workshops, live music, and a butterfly tent. The festival features topiaries inspired by Disney characters, as well as educational shows and demonstrations.

April

Overview:

With Spring Break still continuing, crowds can be high at the beginning of the month but decrease towards the end. Easter is also a big holiday that can cause some crowds. Aside from that, this is a wonderful month to travel, as the weather is beginning to warm up but is still pleasant.

Weather:

The weather in April is much warmer than in the early months, but it's not hot yet. The temperature can range from 70°F to 90°F (21°C to 32°C) during daytime. It could get up to about 60°F (16°C) at night. Compared to other months, it is still not very humid.

Least Crowded Days:

Fewer people are around during the last two weeks of the month than during other weeks.

Most Crowded Days:

The first two weeks of April are usually very busy because everyone is coming off of Spring Break. Easter weekend, which is in April this year, is also a very busy time because all of the schools are out.

Special Event: Easter (April 9, 2023)

Easter is one of the biggest holidays in the United States, and it's also one of the busiest times at Walt Disney World. Observe an Easter-themed parade at the Magic Kingdom. The Easter bunny and rare characters appear in this colorful daytime parade featuring springtime favorites like Mickey, Minnie, Goofy, and Donald.

May

Overview:

May is a very hot month in Florida. Due to the start of the summer season, it is one of the busiest times at Walt Disney World, but the crowds are smaller than they will be during the height of summer.

Weather:

The temperature ranges from 80°F (27°C) to 100°F (38°C) during the daytime. At night, the high may reach the mid-70s (24°C). Storms tend to increase during this time, and it may rain for an hour or so during the day. The rain is only passing showers, so it shouldn't prevent you from traveling.

Least Crowded Days:

The best time to travel is the first two weeks of the month.

Most Crowded Days:

Memorial Day Weekend, which is on March 27-29, 2023

Special Event: Epcot International Flower & Garden Festival (March 1 through July 5, 2023)

Throughout May, you can enjoy the Epcot International Flower & Garden Festival; this annual event will run for the entire month of May, likely ending in early July 2023.

Overview:

June is a bit of a transition month in Florida, where the weather warms up and the summer season starts; however, it's not too hot yet, so crowds are smaller. Crowds are typically light because there aren't many noteworthy events in this month.

Weather:

The temperature ranges from 80°F (27°C) to 100°F (38°C) during the daytime. At night, the high may reach the mid-70°F (24°C). The humidity is medium to high.

Least Crowded Days:

The first Tuesday, Wednesday, and Thursday of the month are the least crowded.

Most Crowded Days:

The last week of June is usually very busy because everyone is coming off their last days of school.

Special Event: Sounds Like Summer Concert Series

With the hot weather, there's no better way to keep cool than with the Sounds Like Summer Concert Series. During this summer concert series, you'll hear a mixture of classical and pop music from different bands and musicians. There will also be live breaks, comedy, and other entertainment.

Overview:

With the summer season starting early, crowds are high during this month, with what seems to be a never-ending line for rides ranging from about 45 minutes to an hour or more. The weather becomes unbearably hot, and visitors worldwide flock to Walt Disney World Resort. Even though July is a busy month, it is a great time to visit water parks and ride the numerous water-themed attractions.

Weather:

The temperature ranges from 90°F (32°C) to 100°F (38°C) during the daytime, but the humidity can make it feel even warmer. The weather stays warm and humid at night, and the high may reach the mid-70°F (24°C).

Least Crowded Days:

There were many empty seats at restaurants, shows, and other attractions during the last week, especially the last three days.

Most Crowded Days:

The first week of April, as the 4th of July falls on a Thursday, so most people will want to stay for the weekend.

Special Event: Concert on The Sky (July 4, 2023)

Celebrate Independence Day with the Concert on the Sky. This event takes place at Disney's Hollywood Studios and features a fireworks show that lights up the sky with popular music and classic American favorites.

August

Overview:

In August, the weather stays hot, and people keep coming until school starts around the middle of the month. Compared to July, August doesn't feel as busy, so if you want to escape the summer heat, this is the best month to choose. Mid-August marks the beginning of Halloween events at the Magic Kingdom. This season, expect to see pumpkins and other autumnal decorations lining Main Street, USA.

Weather:

The temperature ranges from 90°F (32°C) to 100°F (38°C) during the daytime. The weather is sometimes warm and balmy at night, and the high may reach the mid-70s (24°C) to low 80°F (27°C).

Least Crowded Days:

The weekdays in the last two weeks of the month are the least crowded.

Most Crowded Days:

The holiday weekend in mid-August is always very busy because people took their Disney vacation for the week off of work.

Special Event: Epcot International Food and Wine Festival (July 12 - November 18, 2023)

In August, you can enjoy the Epcot International Food and Wine Festival. As you stroll through the International Gateway Pavilion, watch out for Hot Dog with a Twist, where you can make your own hot dog at a kiosk.

September

Overview:

The weather is beginning to cool down in September, and students are heading back to school. The crowds have dwindled, but there are still plenty of kids in the park. This is an ideal time to visit if you are seeking peace and quiet and are not interested in attending

Halloween-themed events. Due to the decline in tourism, the Magic Kingdom will be festooned with Halloween decorations throughout the entire month, and rooms will be available at steep discounts.

Weather:

The temperature varies between 80°F (27°C) and 90°F (32°C) during the day. At night, the high temperature might be around 24°C (70°F). Humidity is between medium and high.

Least Crowded Days:

The weekdays in September are some of the least crowded days.

Most Crowded Days:

Labor Day Weekend (September 5-7, 2023) This is the biggest weekend of the year at Walt Disney World. It is a time for families to visit and spend time together with no worries about lines. This means big crowds, which can sometimes go for as much as 90 minutes, with safety concerns on rides and problems in lines.

Special Event: Epcot International Food and Wine Festival (July 12 - November 18, 2023)

Throughout the entire month of September, you can continue to take advantage of the Epcot International Food and Wine Festival.

October

Overview:

A fan-favorite month, October is the first true fall month in Florida. The temperature gets cooler, and the Halloween celebration begins. This is a great month to visit if you want to avoid the major rush that can come with Halloween events.

Weather:

The temperature ranges from 70°F (21°C) to 80°F (27°C) during the day. The weather stays warm and humid at night, and the high may reach the mid 70°F (24°C). During this time of year, nighttime temperatures begin to get cooler.

Least Crowded Days:

The Tuesdays, Wednesdays, and Thursdays in the first three weeks of this month are the least crowded.

Most Crowded Days:

Halloween and "fall break" (the week before and after Columbus Day) are very busy days at Walt Disney World.

Special Event: Mickey's Not-So-Scary Halloween Party (August 11 -October 31, 2023)

The Halloween Party is a special ticketed event that takes place at Magic Kingdom in the fall.

Guests can see their favorite Disney Villains, a scary parade, and lots of decorations around the park on certain nights from the middle of August until Halloween Day. Guests who pay for separate tickets to these events can also get free candy at "treat spots" throughout the park.

November

Overview:

In November, the weather cools, which draws in vacationers from colder climates. This is one of the most beautiful months at Walt Disney World Resort because the leaves change colors and fall from the trees. Many animals at Animal Kingdom enjoy a great time hunting for food through all of these fallen leaves. The parks feel empty in November, but this is a perfect time to enjoy your favorite rides without waiting for an hour or more in line.

Weather:

The temperature at night is typically around 70°F (21°C), and during the day, it varies from 70°F (21°C) to 80°F (27°C).

Least Crowded Days:

The first week of the month.

Most Crowded Days:

Thanksgiving Week (November 23 - 27, 2023) is a very busy time at Walt Disney World. Families with children in school during this time have arrived for their annual Thanksgiving break and have their entire families staying on site. The traffic congestion is always bad, especially during Thanksgiving week, because of many guests coming to area resorts. Also, Walt Disney World may be busy during Veterans Day (November 11, 2023), but Thanksgiving Week is better.

Special Event: EPCOT International Food and Wine Festival (July 12 - November 18, 2023)

As a whole, the resort doesn't have any big Thanksgiving events. By now, the resort is already set up for Christmas and other winter holidays. You can still enjoy the Epcot International Food and Wine Festival.

December

Overview:

The holidays, including Christmas, are also a big event in Walt Disney World, so the crowds will increase. The resort is nearly always decorated for Christmas and has great holiday events, so this is another favorite month for fans.

Weather:

The temperature ranges from 60°F (15°C) to 80°F (27°C) during the daytime. At night, the high may reach a low of 40°F (4 °C). The humidity is low.

Least Crowded Days:

The first week of the month

Most Crowded Days:

Christmas Week (December 19 - December 30, 2023) It is extremely busy during this holiday week. On certain days, traffic congestion is so bad that people should plan on arriving at least three hours before the posted park opening time to avoid having to stand in more lines. Lines are very long at all of the parks, from early morning until late evening. Primarily because of the Thanksgiving week crowd and then because of Christmas travelers coming in for a two-week break in December, traffic can be very slow. If you are flying in for one day during this time, make sure you arrive early, so you can attend all shows and attractions.

Special Event: Epcot International Festival of the Holidays (November 25th - December 30th, 2023)

Learn about different holiday customs from around the world, indulge in seasonal treats, and maybe even get to meet Santa and Mrs. Claus.

The Most Recommend Months

1. February

The temperature is on the cool side, but not too cold. The weather is still pleasant for walking and is the perfect time for a romantic getaway. Because it's not a holiday month, fewer people with school and work obligations are making their annual trip to Walt Disney World.

The theme parks and hotels will be decorated for Valentine's Day and Presidents' Day. Valentine's week is a good time to visit if you don't mind a little crowd due to special events and decorations, but the last two weeks of the month are the best if you want to avoid crowds.

2. September

In Central Florida, summer lasts until the end of September. Expect hot days and a lot fewer people than in June, July, and August. Most of the month, the Magic Kingdom will be decked out for Halloween. Also new is Mickey's Not-So-Scary Halloween Party. The weekends can get pretty busy, but the weekdays are the least busy, especially on weekdays in early September.

Also, this is the first time it's cooler than 80°F, and the humidity drops a little bit, making for a very comfortable climate. The weather is perfect for taking walks outside or simply enjoying being out in Florida.

3. October

October is the first true fall month in Florida, where the temperature drops and all of the new leaves change colors. Even though Halloween is one of the busier times to visit, it's still a great bet because of the activities and weather. Most people are still in school, so it's also one of the least crowded times to visit. The weather is still warm enough for walking but cool enough to have some precipitation.

You can look forward to decorations, treats, special rides, and Mickey's Not-So-Scary Halloween Party. Be sure to take advantage of the shorter lines and book stays around the Halloween Party.

Least Recommended Months

1. December

December is one of the most popular times to visit Walt Disney World, and for a good reason: Christmas at the resort is incredibly festive. However, this is also one of the most crowded times of year—everyone else has made a point to visit the parks then as well. If you're not interested in celebrating Christmas with the masses, then this is not the time to visit. If you are still determined to visit, check out the Epcot International Festival of the Holidays or Mickey's Very Merry Christmas Party with holiday musical entertainment and tasty treats. Also, ensure you arrive three hours before park opening time to avoid lines and crowds inside the park.

Also, the weather is not great—it's typically in the high 80s (about 30°C) during the day and low 60s (about 15°C) at night, with a lot of humidity. The crowds can make it feel even hotter, which can make walking around uncomfortable. It also tends to rain a little more than usual during this time of year, so make sure to bring an umbrella or a rain jacket.

2. July

The weather is perfect for making frequent trips to the theme parks and walks in the parks, but annoying because of the humidity and heat index. Also, the crowds are much more crowded than usual during this time of year because many people are on vacation or returning from their summer trips. Long lines are expected, which means you might have to wait longer than normal for certain rides and attractions.

If you've never experienced the heat of Central Florida in July, you won't want to go! Summer can be very hot and humid down there, so bring an umbrella or jacket, sunscreen, and other things to wear in case it rains.

If you wish to visit during this time, make sure you visit during a weekday and that the parks will be open for less than two hours. If the parks are busy, schedule your visit for later in the day.

3. August

Similar to July, temperatures are high during the day and low at night. However, August is more humid due to the fact that it's not as dry in Florida during this time of year. Also, because it's summer, there will be a lot of people at the parks. Therefore, you'll have to get used to crowds since there is little time in the day to enjoy visiting them.

The rides can be crowded during this time, too—not only during the day but also for the evening shows and parades. The waterparks can also get very busy with people wanting to cool off after being in the warm Florida weather for hours.

Essential Items to Pack

Knowing the items to pack helps you save space and avoid unnecessary trips to the stores. Especially if you're not a local and need to know where to look for certain items, knowing these items beforehand can save money and also time.

Here are a few of the essentials you'll have to pack (or not have to pack) for your trip:

1. *Planning Book or Sheets*

Having a place to jot down your vacation plans is a great tool to have with you. You can keep your entire itinerary from when you leave to when you return. It's also nice because it can double as a journal of your trip, so years later, you'll be able to reminisce on everything that happened during your vacation.

You can also have it printed beforehand so that you know exactly where and when you will be leaving and when you will be returning. Print out your hotel information so that you can glance to see if it is within walking distance. If not, print the map with all of the names and addresses. Then, print up some information sheets on Disney World so that you'll have some ideas on what to do while at the resort: food, rides, shows, shopping, etcetera.

2. *Bag or Backpack*

You will be traveling a lot, whether you drive to the resort or take the train. Either way, you need something to carry your gear with you. This is where it's useful to have a backpack rather than a suitcase. Backpacks are much more convenient and easy to carry around theme parks. Also, they can't be pulled over on top of you if someone bumps into you, as your suitcase could be.

When traveling with a large group or family, you must consider the size of your backpacks. If you need to transport a large number of items, it may be advantageous for each person to have their own backpack so they can carry everything they need. Take into account how heavy your items are, as well: there's no reason for someone to be lugging around ten pounds if five would suffice. Anything over five pounds should be left behind.

3. *Water Bottle*

A water bottle can be extremely helpful if you don't have one already. With this much walking around the parks, you'll die of thirst, and having a bottle can help when you're thirsty. It's also nice if you're looking to stay hydrated when it's so hot.

If you have a water bottle, be sure it has a sleeve around the bottom. Otherwise, you'll constantly lose your bottle as the bottoms snap off from being walked around. If you're worried about your bottle breaking, then consider getting a water bladder. It holds more than half of the liquid in a regular water bottle and is usually just as expensive or more expensive than a regular water bottle. They are also easier to carry around because they attach to your backpack straps and weigh less than their bottled counterparts. Also, refilling your water bottle can save you a lot of money and time. If you're staying at a hotel, it will have a water fountain where you can fill your bottle.

4. Sunscreen and Bug Spray for Bugs

When visiting an amusement park and traveling around Florida, sunscreen is a necessity. Even if you're the type to tan easily, the sun can be intense in Florida due to the humidity and heat index. Because of this, people who normally burn in the sun get much darker when they visit Florida. If you need to be tanner, sunscreen will give you some color while protecting your skin from cancer-causing UV rays. The sunscreen should be non-greasy and have a good amount of SPF in it so that you do not burn from the sun after being in the park for hours.

Bug spray is another necessity; there are a lot of mosquitos at Disney World for some reason. Those who have allergies to bug bites and get huge welts from them should be especially aware. Spray the bug spray on you ahead of time so that you don't get bit while walking around the park and end up with a bunch of itchy red bumps all over your body. The bug spray should be chemical-free, containing no DEET or other chemicals that can harm your health and the environment.

5. Sunglasses and Hats

It's very bright in Florida, especially during the summertime. Sunglasses can be pricey, but they can save you a lot of money over time. The sun's rays can damage your eyes, so wearing sunglasses is a great way to protect your eyes and look stylish. Be sure to get a pair that will fit comfortably around your head and sit tightly, so they don't fall off when walking around the amusement park. If you know you're going to be outside a lot during the day, then it may be best to get a pair of polarized glasses. They are more expensive but will help if it rains, or your eyes begin to hurt from the sun.

Hats are also very helpful, especially if you're not a fan of the sun. Hats can protect your head from the heat while also providing you with some shade. In Florida, it's not uncommon to be in a park during a scorching hot day and still experience bone-chilling temps at night that drop to around zero. A hat will make your head more comfortable and protect you from the cold air. If you do not want to worry about your hair getting ruined while walking around in the humidity, especially if you're going to be spending most of your time in the parks and in water, then a hat is the perfect way to keep your hair from getting all tangled and messy. Hats are also very inexpensive, so there's no reason not to have one.

6. Comfortable Shoes

Comfort is key when you're going to be walking around the parks all day long. There's nothing worse than having sore feet at the end of your vacation because your shoes are hurting you. For girls, you should have at least one pair of shoes that are fairly flat. If you're wearing heels all day long, you'll be in a lot of pain at the end of the day. Even if your flats are uncomfortable and rub against your feet, it will be better than wearing high heels all day long.

There are a variety of brands and styles of shoes, so you're bound to find something that's comfortable to walk around in. If you're more of a mall girl and aren't used to walking around all day long with your shoes on, then try going shopping for new comfy shoes ahead of time and wearing them around the house or work to break them in.

Boys can wear any shoes they want while they're in the parks as long as they aren't uncomfortable and make their feet bleed. Athletic shoes with padding and arch support are good choices, as well as some flip-flops if you're looking to keep your feet a bit cooler. If you have flat feet, your best bet is to get a pair of inserts for your shoes to help with the pain in your feet.

7. Rain Poncho or Umbrella

Florida is known for being very rainy, and it's not uncommon to see rain falling from the sky during the summertime. The rain can make it difficult to walk around and ruin your day by forcing everyone inside for a few hours before going out again. People who want their trip protected from bad weather should bring a small rain poncho or umbrella. The ponchos are cheap and come in a variety of colors. It's a good idea to get a rain poncho that'll help you hide from the rain so that people won't be able to see you leaking water all over the place. If you anticipate rain, it may be prudent to purchase a watertight umbrella; this way, you won't have to worry about getting your belongings wet.

Of course, it may not always be raining at Disney World, and there can still be bad weather, so having an umbrella might not be necessary for everyone, but it's good to have one or two in your bag if needed. If you're looking for something much sturdier and better quality, then waterproof umbrellas are what you should be looking for. They have a better material so that it doesn't break easily, keep your things dry in the rain, etc., and are also way more stylish than a poncho.

8. Phone

You'll need to call your airline, theme park, and resort reservations, as well as the local phone numbers you will have at the resort in case of an accident or any other trouble while at the parks. There are pay phones that you can use at Disney World, but they're only at specific locations and often need more money. It's also a good idea for you to have your own phone that has an internet connection on it so that you can use it to check your email and search for prices online ahead of time.

Not only is having a phone convenient, but it's also great for taking photos and videos of your vacation. Most phones have cameras that are in HD quality, which is great for taking photos and videos of the rides, characters, and other objects of interest at Disney World. You can upload them to your computer and share them with family and friends online when you get home.

9. ID and Credit Cards (and cash if needed)

Everyone is required to show a photo ID at all of the parks and also at the resorts and hotels. You will need to have your ID with you if you want to get into any of the parks and your resort room. If you purchase anything while on vacation, you'll also have to show your ID. Security may ask you to see an ID from anyone over 21 so that they can check to see if they are allowed into a park (and also a lot of bars). Having a credit card is also a good idea when you're looking for souvenirs or want to grab something from one of the stores in the parks.

Having cash on hand is also advisable, especially if you plan to purchase souvenirs. You can purchase many souvenirs at the parks, but many of them will set you back by more than $10, and it's very difficult to pay that much money at Disney World. Because of this, the only way to make sure you get your money's worth out of shopping on your trip is to have cash on hand. This way, you can return everything without being charged a huge amount for something that got damaged in shipping.

10. Camera and Film/Memory Cards

Taking pictures and videos at Disney World will be one of the most important things you do on your trip. While having a phone as your camera may be convenient, having a good camera with film or a memory card is much better. It allows you to take more photos and videos than you would with a phone and also capture more memories of your time at Disney World. A good camera can also endure a lot of use, as many of the rides and attractions at Disney World will make your camera work hard throughout the day.

When you are considering what camera to buy, you will want to look at reviews and comparisons of different cameras to find the one that suits your needs best. Not only is it important to purchase a high-quality camera, but it's also advisable to examine the lenses and memory card that come with it. A lot of cameras come with a kit lens, but most people end up using their own lenses anyway, so it's a good idea to make sure that you buy a camera that includes the best lenses you'd want to use in the parks.

11. Extra Batteries/Power Banks

If you want to ensure that your phone remains charged while visiting the parks, you should purchase extra batteries so that you can swap them out as needed and continue capturing all of your priceless memories. While charging stations are available in the parks, a lot of people have found that the power outlets are only sometimes in convenient places. You can also charge your phone when you're at the hotel or eating dinner if you have a portable charger or power bank. The power banks cost money, but they are well worth it if you run low on juice throughout your trip.

You don't have to worry about carrying around the charger for your camera because it's not very big, but it's a good idea to have extra batteries for your phone. If you're doing a lot of photography, you're going to want to ensure that your phone is working and taking pictures at all times throughout the day. There are also charging stations at the parks, but if you want to save some time, it might be best to charge up your phone on your own so that you can spend more time at the parks and less time charging up your phone.

12. First Aid Kit

Being prepared for any emergencies that may arise during your trip to Disney World is a very important part of going on vacation. This means you should ensure you have some first aid supplies before you go. The best thing about having a first aid kit is that it can save lives, but it also gives you the peace of mind of knowing that if something does happen in the parks, then you'll be able to take care of yourself and other passengers at the resort when necessary. It's also great to put together a first aid kit ahead of time so that you know exactly what's inside and how much prep work needs to be done ahead of time in case someone gets hurt at Disney World.

While there are first aid kits inside most of the larger hotels at Disney World, it's also a good idea to bring your own first aid kit to the parks. The parks don't give first aid kits to visitors, so it's best to always have one with you in case something goes wrong. You can either buy a small first aid kit ahead of time and keep it with you in your bag, or you can purchase a larger one from Walgreens or CVS that will contain more supplies than what may be available at the parks.

13. Ziploc Bags

Having Ziploc bags on hand is just one way that you can stay prepared for all of your adventures at Disney World. They are extremely useful and will save you a lot of money if you ever need to replace something because it got wet or ruined from a rainstorm. If you have an umbrella or a raincoat, then using Ziploc bags as an extra layer of protection is a great idea. When it rains at Disney World, it will rain extremely hard, and you'll need to stay dry in order to enjoy the rest of your day at the park. There are plenty of times when you'll want to bring snacks into one of the parks, and having Ziploc bags will allow you to not worry about bringing any bag inside with you so that you can just put them right into your back pocket or bag once they're fully dry again.

You'll also want some Ziploc bags if you plan on taking anything back home with you after your trip to Disney World. There is a lot of merchandise that you may want to buy, but it's only sometimes good to bring it home in the bag that it came in. Having Ziploc bags on hand is a quick way to put items like small stuffed animals or shirts into so that they don't get ruined by everything else in your bag. You can even make sure you have Ziploc bags for your food if there's ever a time when Disney stops selling its branded plastic covering bags.

14. Hand Sanitizer

Another thing that you'll want to take with you is some hand sanitizer. While washing your hands before meals is a great idea, sometimes the bathrooms are far away, and washing your hands after every meal is impossible. Having some hand sanitizer on you will allow you to clean your hands and make sure that they don't get contaminated by germs and bacteria by the time you sit down to eat.

While Walt Disney World will often have hand sanitizer dispensers in the restrooms if they are available, it's always a good idea to have some of your own on hand, just in case. You can also purchase hand sanitizer from a pharmacy before you go and ensure you have enough for the entire trip.

15. Wet Wipes

Another thing that you'll definitely want on hand is some wet wipes. The hotels provide towels for you to use, but sometimes it just doesn't feel like enough, and you want to be able to clean off after a hot day spent in the park. A wet wipe will allow you to freshen up whenever you need to, which is the best part about them since they don't take up much room. They're also useful if you need to clean sticky hands and faces before eating a meal or portion out snacks for younger children or picky eaters on your trip.

Wet wipes are very useful at Disney World because they can be used not just on yourself but also on your other passengers as well if needed. Your guests can use them in order to wash their hands after eating, and you can also use them to help clean up the table when you're finished with your meal. Your wet wipes are also great for wiping down the stroller during nap time. Many of the strollers are very popular, and there will likely be lots of people using them over the course of your trip, so it's best to keep everything nice and clean before you hand it off to someone else.

16. Tums or Pepto Bismol

Tums itself is an antacid that can be used as a bring-all medicine if you're having heartburn or indigestion. You'll be eating out quite a bit during your trip, so having some of this on hand for any stomach upset you might have will be helpful. Pepto Bismol is another great medicine for upset stomachs, but it's also helpful for diarrhea as well. It does not take up much space, so it is a great item to bring along if you need something for stomach or digestive problems.

Even if you know that everything will be fine, it's still a good idea to bring any medications or anti-nausea drugs you might need on your trip. You can never be sure when any illness will strike, and it could help to have some of these things on hand in case it does happen.

17. Ear Plugs

If you're a light sleeper or you have children who like to play in the hallway outside of your room, having some earplugs with you will be useful. If you're trying to sleep, it can be difficult to hear someone walking outside your room, but having some earplugs on hand will help you block out any noise and ensure you can get a good sleep in your hotel room almost every night.

Not only that, but the hotels are constantly getting loud at Disney World because there are so many people in many places simultaneously. When it's time to go to sleep, you may not be able to sleep soundly without a pair of earplugs. Ear plugs are also useful because you can use them if you're sleeping in a resort that has fireworks every night. Some people love the fireworks, and others hate them, so having earplugs on hand is a great way to ensure you can find the right amount of sleep you need to feel great throughout the rest of your day at the parks.

18. Baby Powder or Gold Bond Medicated Body Powder

Having baby powder or Gold Bond medicated body powder on hand will help you keep your feet dry after a long day at the parks. The first part of Disney World that you visit is going to be very hot and humid, which means that your feet will sweat a lot during the day. You can use the baby powder to keep your feet smelling fresh between showers, and it can also help you avoid blisters on your feet if you're wearing new shoes or boots on your trip.

It's always a good idea to bring baby powder to Disney World with you because it's something that almost everyone uses every single day when they get out of the shower. It's a quick and cheap way to keep your feet dry during the day, which can help you avoid any issues with blisters that might occur in your shoes and boots.

19. Chapstick or Lip Balm

Lip balm is a great thing to have on hand for most of your trip because it's something that's constantly going to need to be re-applied. Even if you're not in hot weather, your lips constantly move when you talk and eat, which means you can get irritated very easily. Having some lip balm will help prevent any issues from happening during your trip and can also help to make sure that you're feeling good throughout the rest of the day as well.

20. Duct Tape or Zip Ties

Duct tape is an amazing thing to have on hand because it can be used in a variety of ways. Wristbands will most likely break over your trip, so you'll want to keep some duct tape with you in case of one break while you're out at the parks. It's also useful if you're in need of a quick fix for broken items, like a broken zipper or torn raincoat.

Zip ties are another great item for your trip because they can be used in many ways. One way that zip ties can be used is to hang up your clothes after removing them from the dryer at the resort, which helps keep things organized and clean. They're also useful as a temporary fix if you have any broken straps on any suitcases or bags you're traveling with. You could even use them to keep all of your cords together and organized if they still need to be stored inside a specific bag or compartment on one of your bags or luggage.

If you're going on a vacation to Disney World, you'll want to ensure that you have these things on hand to make your trip as smooth and easy as possible. You don't necessarily need these items all the time, but they will certainly be useful at some point when you're at Disney World enjoying the park with your family and friends.

Transportation Options

With the exception of a few Disney World Resorts and theme parks, travel between locations at Walt Disney World requires the use of some form of transportation. When you consider all the available modes of transportation throughout the Resort, you will want to try them all at some point during your vacation.

The following different options are available to you:

1. Airport Shuttle

There are multiple options for transportation between the Orlando International Airport (MCO) and your Walt Disney World Resort hotel, as well as select hotels in the surrounding area.

Some of the different ways to get from the Airport to your hotel are as follows:

a. Mears Connect

Mears Connect is now taking care of hotels near Disney that Disney's Magical Express used to take care of. The first shuttle service between Orlando International Airport and Disney resorts began on January 1, 2022. A traveler who utilizes this service will board a motor coach bus, van, or car at the airport and be driven to their designated Walt Disney World Resort area hotel with their luggage. You will share your ride with other guests and make stops at other resort hotels en route.

The prices listed below are "introductory," meaning they could change anytime:

STANDARD SERVICE	ADULTS	CHILD(3-9 years old)
ONE WAY	$16	$13.50
ROUND TRIP	$32	$27

Standard service is shared between big and small vehicles, wait times are kept track of, and there are fewer stops. You have to make a reservation for airport transportation; it won't be set up for you automatically. You must make reservations on the official Mears Connect website, as this cannot be added to your Disney World vacation package.

Express service is available, but it can only be reserved for round trips. The price is $250 (subject to change) for up to 4 people, and each extra person costs $55. The standard service has a rate for children, but the express service does not. The number of guests should include children of all ages. Express service has short wait times and gives direct service. It is not a private service.

b. The Sunshine Flyer

It is a motorcoach bus with a theme that transports guests from Orlando International Airport to the Walt Disney World Resorts. The service is a convenient and inexpensive way to get to Disney, so guests can start having fun on their vacation as soon as they step off the plane. Their buses are new, high-quality motorcoaches with designs based on old train engines and passenger cars. From the way the buses look to the people who work on them dressed as conductors and engineers from the 1920s, the motorcoaches are like time machines that let you see how people traveled by train in the 1920s. There are some buses that are themed as vintage railroad cars that look like the actual passenger cars from the 1920s. It is available year-round but runs during peak summer travel months and holidays.

It is a shared service, so there are no private vehicles and no seat belts on these buses, only a lap belt to hold your child in place. For safety purposes, you should be able to sit next to an adult without them being too close. If it's raining or snow is expected, the bus may not take you. In that case, the bus operator will tell you to find another way.

You have to buy tickets for The Sunshine Flyer at least four days before you want to ride it. Go to www.sunshineflyer.com to find out more and book tickets.

c. Private Ground Transportation

Private ground transportation between Orlando International Airport and Walt Disney World Resort is now available. There are a number of choices, such as luxury vans, sedans, SUVs, executive limousines, and stretch limousines. You can book this direct, private ground transportation up to five days before your arrival.

Your Dreams Unlimited Travel agent can add round-trip transportation to your package from Orlando International Airport to a Walt Disney World Resort hotel. Up to one complimentary car seat is available for children under the age of five, with the availability of additional car seats dependent on supply.

The airport shuttle is a convenient way to travel between the airport and your hotel. There may be more comfortable ways of travel, but it's a lot more affordable than if you had to rent a car or take a cab.

2. Skyliner

Image: Jedi94 at English Wikipedia

Skyliner is the only way to get to EPCOT or Hollywood Studios from Disney's Caribbean Beach Resort, Disney's Riviera Resort, Disney's Pop Century Resort, or Disney's Art of

Animation Resort. Buses can only be used when Skyliner is not running (which often happens in the summer due to weather). If you are staying in the EPCOT Resort area, you can walk or take a Friendship Boat or ride the Skyliner. This gives the impression that guests are riding with their Disney friends. Each gondola shines in one of eight bright colors and has smooth, curved lines that make it easy to spot from above.

The Epcot International Gateway, Disney's Hollywood Studios, Pop Century, Art of Animation, and Disney's Riviera Resort all have gondola stations. Disney's Caribbean Beach Resort serves as the HUB. Disney Skyliner Gondolas will stop at each station, so you'll never miss a stop again. Each cabin has a glass floor and see-through mesh sides so you can see the beauty of nature below as you glide to your destination. The gondolas also have overhead luggage storage, allowing guests to bring all their belongings with them on their journey. The best thing about the Disney Skyliner Gondolas is that they are completely free to ride. Just hop on, sit back, and enjoy the views as you glide over trees and sparkling blue water to your destination.

Disney Skyliner Approximate Travel Times:

DESTINATION	TRAVEL TIME
Disney's Caribbean Beach Resort to Disney's Hollywood Studios	6 minutes
Disney's Caribbean Beach Resort to Disney's Pop Century Resort or Disney's Art of Animation Resort	6 minutes
Disney's Caribbean Beach Resort to Disney's Riviera Resort	5 minutes
Disney's Riviera Resort to International Gateway at Epcot	9 minutes
Disney's Caribbean Beach Resort to International Gateway at Epcot	15 minutes

Plan extra time if you want to switch between Pop Century and Art of Animation at the Skyliner station that serves both parks. Since you have to switch lines at the Caribbean Beach station, you'll have to get off and go to the back of a different line for wherever you're going.

The lines at the Riviera station may be longer in both directions because most people pass through the station without getting off. It may take longer for an empty gondola to come through the station than at the other stations, where there are always empty cabins.

3. Monorail System

Anthony Quintano from Westminster, United States

At first, the monorail system connected the Contemporary and Polynesian hotels to the Magic Kingdom and the Transportation and Ticket Center. The current model of monorail began running in 1990, and by early 1991, all 12 of them were in use. The Mark VI can hold more people and has better air conditioning, door systems, and safety features than the Mark V. There are six cars on each Mark VI train. The whole thing is 203 feet long and can hold 365 people.

The track consists of precast concrete beams with a width of 26 inches that are supported by concrete columns spaced approximately 50 feet apart. Each monorail moves on rubber tires and is powered by eight 112-horsepower DC motors on each side of the beam, which is part of a 600-volt DC drive system. The 13.6-mile monorail system will take more than 150,000 people to the Magic Kingdom and Epcot parks every day, on average.

Operating hours:

The first monorail departure is thirty minutes prior to the opening of the first park. The last monorail departs one hour after the closing of the last park.

Most Magic Kingdom guests will be able to ride the Disney monorail. To access the park from the Magic Kingdom's main parking lot, guests must take the monorail or ferry boat. Wait at a designated Monorail stop location for the train to arrive and open its doors. The monorail's entrance and exit are typically located in the same area.

The Walt Disney World monorail is free and open to all guests without a ticket. If you wish to park and take the Resort Monorail to the Magic Kingdom or Epcot, you may be required to pay a parking fee.

4. Boats

Walt Disney World Water Transportation makes getting where you want to go easy. They offer water launch, boat, and ferryboat services. There are different kinds of boats that go to different places in the Magic Kingdom, Disney Springs, and Epcot. Water transportation at Disney is always going to be a little slower than a bus or car. Still, it's one of a kind and very Disney.

The following are types of boats (and ferries) you can take to get around on:

a. Magic Kingdom

i. Ferry Boats

Photo by: Brian Petz

The ferry is a great way to see the Magic Kingdom and the area around it. Two identical Magic Kingdom class ferries transport guests daily between the Transportation and Ticket Center and Magic Kingdom.

Capacity and Schedule:

Each ferryboat can accommodate 600 passengers and three crew members. During the opening and closing periods, all three ferries operate. During daytime and late night hours, two ferries typically operate with wait times between 10 and 20 minutes.

The Magic Kingdom Ferry typically begins service 45 minutes prior to park opening and continues for up to one hour after park closing. If Magic Kingdom offers early theme park admission benefits, the ferry will begin service approximately 45 minutes prior to the start of these hours. Likewise, extended evening hours for parties and after-hours events are permitted. It takes approximately 15 minutes to board, cross, and dock the Magic Kingdom Ferry.

After entering the Transportation and Ticket Center, the ferry boat dock is located to the far left. After the ferry returns from its return trip and unloads its passengers, a cast member will open the gate for new guests to board. You may then board the ferry and decide whether to remain on the main deck or ascend to the upper deck. However, seating on the ferry could be much better. Therefore, snag a seat as soon as possible if you require one.

b. Disney's Hollywood Studios and Epcot

i. FriendShip Boats

Michael Miley from Schaumburg, USA

These boats are a slow but pleasant mode of transportation across Seven Seas Lagoon and between EPCOT's International Gateway and Disney's Hollywood Studios. Each FriendShip Boat offers both standing and seated space for approximately 100 passengers.

Schedule:

The FriendShip Boats begin running every day, around 8:30 a.m. until around 60 minutes after Disney Park close. The boat ride between the two parks, which includes all stops along the way, lasts about 25 minutes.

Disney Friendship Boats Route:

First, we'll examine the Friendship Boats that connect Epcot and Hollywood Studios. These boats stop at each area resort between the two parks in a specific order.

The Friendship Boat route travels in the direction indicated below.

From Hollywood Studios to Epcot via the Friendship Boat Route:

- Disney's Hollywood Studios
- Swan and Dolphin Hotel (includes Swan Reserve)
- Disney's Yacht and Beach Club Resort (One Stop)
- Disney's Boardwalk Inn
- Epcot

Route of the Friendship Boats from Epcot to Hollywood Studios:

- Epcot
- Disney's Boardwalk Inn
- Disney's Beach and Yacht Club (One Stop)
- Swan and Dolphin Hotel (includes Swan Reserve)
- Disney's Hollywood Studios

You should be careful to get in the right line when boarding a boat from the dock at your resort.

Boat Landings:

The following locations serve as the FriendShip Boat landings for EPCOT, Disney's Hollywood Studios, and the EPCOT Resort hotels:

- The EPCOT International Gateway

Can be reached by exiting World Showcase between the United Kingdom and France Pavilions. Maintain your left position as you pass through the EPCOT exit.

- Disney's BoardWalk Inn

This boat landing, also referred to as Promenade Pier, is located in the center of the Disney BoardWalk, in front of the Disney's BoardWalk Inn's lawn. Use the line on the right side for EPCOT and the line on the left side for Disney's Hollywood Studios.

- Disney's Yacht & Beach Club

This boat landing is located on the lighthouse pier in front of Disney's Yacht Club Resort. For EPCOT, use the left lane, and for Disney's Hollywood Studios, use the right lane.

- Walt Disney World Swan & Dolphin Resorts

Locate the boat dock in the middle of the two hotels' walkways. Utilize the right lane for Disney's Hollywood Studios and the left lane for EPCOT.

- Disney's Hollywood Studios

The covered boat landing walkway can be found by heading towards Lake Hollywood after leaving the Disney theme park and taking the path that leads to the right.

Make sure to check the displays along these piers for the accurate time of arrival. If you are unable to locate a sign displaying the time, ask an employee for assistance. The Friendship Boats are an excellent means of transportation within the Epcot Resorts area. They are particularly useful if you are unfamiliar with the area or if this is your first visit.

c. Disney Springs

Water Taxi service between Marketplace, Pleasure Island, and West Side operates every 20 minutes from 10:30 a.m. to 4:30 p.m. and every 10 minutes from 4:30 p.m. to 1:30 a.m. Every 20 minutes throughout the day, the boat leaves from Disney's Saratoga Springs Resort & Spa, Treehouse Villas, and Disney's Old Key West Resort.

The operating hours vary based on water and weather conditions. Note that Disney watercraft do not permit any luggage or alcohol. Each and every stroller must be folded and stowed out of the aisle. For disabled Guests, medical strollers will be treated as wheelchairs.

Minnie Vans are considered one of the most versatile transportation services available in Walt Disney World, and they offer a more efficient way to travel than relying on the complimentary Disney's Magical Express service. Whether you are embarking on an excursion or exploring Walt Disney World, Minnie Vans can transport you between Orlando International Airport, your Disney Resort hotel, and anywhere on Walt Disney World property.

Other Mode of Transportation

Depending on your origin, driving your own vehicle may be more convenient, especially if you are staying on the property. You can travel in the comfort of your own vehicle without having to rely on Disney's transportation services. Consider renting a car from the Orlando International Airport if driving to Orlando is not practical. Especially due to the absence of Disney's Magical Express, you would be responsible for your own transportation throughout Disney World. While there is a nightly fee for self-parking at all Disney hotels, general parking at the theme parks is complimentary for hotel guests (and annual pass holders).

If you are not staying on-site, compare the costs of ride-sharing services to those of a rental car, hotel parking fees, and general parking fees at the theme parks. It would depend on how far away your hotel is and how many people are traveling with you. Also, consider your proximity to Disney Springs; if you can walk to Disney Springs, you can board any of the resort buses there (though you'll need to transfer buses if you're headed to the theme parks).

Navigating The Parks

Navigating Walt Disney World can be overwhelming for both first-time and repeat visitors. Knowing how to navigate the parks is important if you wish to avoid the lines and maximize your efficiency.

1. Plan Ahead of Time

One of the keys to avoiding major Disney World mistakes is to acquire as much local knowledge as possible. How does one plan for a location they have never visited? You can find maps of Disney Parks on Disney's website, and it doesn't hurt to familiarize yourself with the park layouts. Disney is large, and while it is always amazing to be at Disney World, an easier way to navigate is a familiar location that you are comfortable with. If you know how the park layout works, you will know your destination's direction and can use your freedom of movement to maneuver within the park.

Determine if you want to use Disney transportation or if you will be driving yourself. If you're planning to drive on Disney property, familiarize yourself with Google Maps and Waze, which are apps that can be easily downloaded on your smartphone. Park hours or days may change from year to year or during special events, so it is important you verify the hours before you go. And if you wish to avoid being responsible for navigating Disney property? Plan to use Disney's transportation services! Thus, you can relax and rely on someone else to navigate Disney World for you.

Understand that Walt Disney World is enormous. We are talking about city-sized proportions. As a result, getting around requires time. As you decide which Disney Theme Parks to visit and where to eat, keep in mind that the travel time between your Walt Disney World Resort hotel and a Disney Park can take up to an hour.

There is nothing "quick" about traveling throughout Walt Disney World. Although Disney's transportation is excellent, the park's size makes getting around more time-consuming. Keeping this in mind, be sure to account for travel time. Allow yourself additional time to reach your reservations in order to avoid stress and missing important events. As you plan, remember that anything can happen. Your transportation service could be late, get lost, or get stuck in traffic. You must allow yourself time to prepare for this potential delay. If there is an attraction that you wish to experience but is far away from your destination, consider taking a break and resting at a nearby location before continuing on the rest of your route.

2. Pack Your Patience

Remember to pack your patience. One of the hardest things about visiting Disney World is the crowds and long lines. The wait times for each ride, show, and restaurant can vary depending on the time of day. In addition, the park's size makes navigation difficult. With all these factors in mind, you must be able to enjoy yourself despite waiting in endless lines. If you do not wish to deal with the crowd or any other unforeseen circumstances, then Walt Disney World is not for you.

The key to this tip is that it requires patience. Patience is simply the ability to endure or remain calm while waiting. As a result, one of the major mistakes that people who have never visited Disney World make is they expect everything to go smoothly without any complications. They think that once they arrive at a Disney Park, everything there should go exactly as planned and without a hitch. This, of course, is not the case. Everyone knows that nothing can go perfectly.

When you are not happy or feel overwhelmed by the crowds, take a moment to breathe and remember that everyone else is feeling the same way. If you are able to control your emotions, no one will know how stressed you are. Every stressful situation is made easier with that extra layer of patience. If you can learn how to use this tool, you will soon be able to deal with the crowds at Walt Disney World and other stressful situations in your daily life.

3. Know When To Escape

Sometimes, you will have time to wait in lines and still have time to accomplish what you wanted to do before entering Disney Park. However, in some instances, you may want to skip the lines and see Disney World attractions at a less-crowded time. For example, to avoid crowds, if you intend to watch the Magic Kingdom fireworks, get in line for transportation while the show is still in progress. Sure, you'll miss a portion of the fireworks, but you'll also avoid the massive crowd surge that follows! Alternatively, you could wait until after the show has concluded and the initial large influx of guests has left the park. Typically, buses run for at least an hour after the park closes, so you'll have some time to let the crowds for transportation subside before you board the bus.

If you have your heart set on a specific attraction and it is not at all crowded, do not stand in line simply because everyone else is doing so. As long as it fits into your vacation plans, there's no harm in visiting a park specifically to be able to experience an attraction that is less of a crowd-pleaser. Make sure that you're aware of the park hours before you arrive so you can figure out how much time you'll need at that park before heading to another.

If the weather looks like it might rain or an event is scheduled at Disney World and crowds are expected, consider changing your schedule to avoid the chaos and remaining lines. If you're at a park that is closing, ride what you can before the park closes and then leave.

This tip is all about knowing when to put in the hard work and when to save yourself some time. If you are trying to fit everything into one day, but your schedule is jam-packed, be sure not to let anyone pressure you into doing something just because it's "what's right." It is perfectly acceptable to leave a park if you've had a long day and don't want to do something you know will result in tired legs and a sore back. Make sure that what you leave is one that you would want to visit again and revisit in the future. Each park has its own unique atmosphere, so be sure to choose which parks give you the best experience for your needs.

4. Prepare Your Body

You will walk a lot during your visit. Even if you don't intend to begin with, you'll find yourself walking between the Disney theme parks or randomly throughout the grounds of Walt Disney World Resort at some point. When you are in a hurry, it is easy to forget how long and strenuous it can be to walk on vacation. Dress comfortably with loose-fitting clothing and comfortable shoes. Overly tight or too-small clothes will make you uncomfortable and distract you from the joy of your trip. You can be sure that if you are uncomfortable, then it will make others around you feel just as uncomfortable.

Wear socks that insulate your feet from hot surfaces. You never know where you might step, so it is best to prevent the possibility of a burn by wearing something on the bottom of your feet. Be sure to take some time to rest and find a place with shade during the hottest hours of the day if you have difficulty regulating your body temperature when outside. Also, carry water and snacks with you if you are walking long distances.

Even if you exercise regularly at home, a Florida vacation can be much more physically demanding than usual. It's not uncommon for people to feel sore just from walking around the park! To avoid this, it is best that you are well-rested when you visit Walt Disney World resort to ensure that you have enough energy to take in the wonders of each park. If you are traveling a long distance to get there, get enough sleep and eat healthy meals to prepare for Disney World.

Walt Disney World is a magical place. Even though it's packed with tourists and long lines, something about Walt Disney World makes you want to keep coming back. Because of the wonder of Walt Disney World, guests are returning for more. So, make sure to pack your positive attitude and have fun during your next visit! Walt Disney World can be overwhelming at times, but if you take each day as it comes and make the most out of it, everything will turn out just fine.

TIPS FOR BOOKING AND PLANNING

One of the most enchanted vacation spots on Earth is Walt Disney World. However, it can also be difficult, pricey, and stressful. With that said, you need to know how to get the best Disney World deal possible. There are plenty of tips out there to help you save money on your vacation, but many of them can cost you time, money, and headaches, too.

Timing is Key - When to Book

You'll want to do your research before booking a Walt Disney World vacation. Many times throughout the year, you can save a lot of money on your vacation, but you must know when to be at home to take advantage of these deals. A big sale may sound like a great opportunity to save money, but it may be useful if you're away and ready to book in the long run.

With Disney World vacations, it is unquestionably advantageous to plan ahead. Disney gives the best discounts to those who make reservations in advance because it needs to staff hotels, restaurants, theme park attractions, and transportation. The best discounts are often offered three to six months in advance. Because Disney World is such a popular destination, planning ahead also allows you to reserve the hotel and restaurants of your choice, ensuring a great experience.

As a general rule, you should book your vacation at least four to six months in advance. To ensure you receive the best deal, book as far in advance as possible without booking so far in advance that you forget or miss out on vacation deals. Good deals may be hard to find if you wait until the last minute. In addition, when traveling far to get to Walt Disney World, it's a huge disappointment if your travel plans are held up due to the unavailability of accommodations. If you book early enough, you may also be forced to stay in hotels farther from the park or outside the gates of Walt Disney World. While staying outside of the resort may save you some money on your vacation, it can also make getting to and from the parks a pain.

Where Are the Best Deals?

While there are many different websites that advertise Disney World deals, your best bet is to check out the Walt Disney World official website. This is the place that Disney employees check daily and generally offers a competitive price. If you need more than this to help you determine what deal works best for you, you can also check out specific sites such as Undercover Tourist, which provides great information and reviews of several travel sites.

One great way to save money on your Disney vacation is to purchase a multi-day ticket that includes water parks, sports complexes, and other recreational facilities with Walt Disney World in addition to the theme parks themselves. The ticket will still be a multi-day pass, but it can be used at all the attractions and provide a nice break. While this deal may not save you money on a single day in the parks, you will have access to more things for fewer dollars in the long run.

How Long Should I Stay?

The number of days you stay at Walt Disney World is also a big factor you should consider when purchasing your Disney vacation. While staying longer or shorter will not likely save you money on your vacation, it will significantly alter your overall experience.

1. 1 to 3 Days

Since there are four theme parks (Magic Kingdom, Epcot, Disney's Hollywood Studios, and Animal Kingdom) and two water parks, so a day up to 3 days typically involve choosing one or two parks over the others. Since you cannot do everything, you must decide what you can do, enjoy it to the fullest, and let go of the things you cannot do. Even though you can start in one park and end in another, you still need at least eight hours of uninterrupted time in a single park to maximize your day. You can definitely do Magic Kingdom and go on one ride, but to make it count, you want to be there for the park opening. For those who want to start their day early at Epcot and then do Hollywood Studios or vice versa, it makes sense as long as you are spending at least 6 hours in any one park.

While there is no one way to travel to Walt Disney World, the typical time frame is a quick trip of just a few days. If you add up the hours you spend in different parks each day and make sure that you include rides and stops for meals, you need about 10 hours per park per day. The majority of attractions are open well into the evening, which is good news. So if the Magic Kingdom crowd thinned out by eight p.m., your best bet would be to hop on the monorail to Hollywood Studio and check out some of the shows or take a boat ride through the resort lagoon. You may want to take a quick jaunt toward Downtown Disney for some more shopping or eating. You could head back to the Magic Kingdom for the rest of the day, go on just one ride, and then catch the afternoon parade.

2. 4 to 5 Days

This trip length is ideal for the majority of people because it allows them to visit all four Disney World theme parks and possibly spend a second day at their favorite park while also fitting within their work vacation limits. Though this kind of trip may include a day at the beach or visits to other nearby attractions, most people in this category are planning a Disney vacation rather than combining Disney with another type of vacation. The price per day of your theme park admission ticket decreases with each additional day you visit. This length of the trip will provide a lot of fun and make you feel as if you've been to Disney World, but it will leave you wanting more.

If you are only staying for four or five days and planning on visiting more than one theme park in a single day, this could be very tiring for everyone involved. The best way to avoid boredom is to make sure there is something new to experience daily. If your plan is to spend a fourth of your trip at Epcot while the rest at Magic Kingdom and Animal Kingdom, chances are that you may be bored with Disney World by the end of your stay.

One way around this problem is by planning the trip with lots of shorter trips; this way, things will feel fresh even after a few days. This could include two full days at Magic Kingdom followed by a day at Animal Kingdom, a day at Disney's Hollywood Studios, and then one final full day at the Magic Kingdom. By breaking up the parks into short trips, you will give each park more attention but still be able to get a taste of everything.

3. 6 Days Plus

If 4-to-5-day trips make you feel like you've been to Disney World, then 6-day or longer trips make you feel like you've been on a resort vacation. The extra time allows you to balance enjoyment and rest better. Longer trips also allow you to revisit your favorite parks and attractions, but with more time to explore and experience everything Disney World offers. This is an excellent option for summer travel, especially for those traveling with young children or elderly relatives. Longer trips also provide greater flexibility for those with tight work schedules. While you are likely tempted to cram as much fun into your vacation as possible, packing in a ton of activities may become overwhelming. Longer trips give you the opportunity to take it easy and do some of the less exciting things that are still enjoyable.

The downside to this length of the trip is that it can become expensive. While you may begin with an excellent value ticket, you will quickly accrue additional charges for parking, transportation to and from the parks, food, souvenirs, and other related expenses. On top of that, longer trips require more time away from work and other daily activities, which can be costly in terms of both time and money. If you decide to take a longer trip, make sure you plan breaks with less activity each day so that you can enjoy the parks with energy and enthusiasm. The trick is to not let any one day ruin the whole experience. Take advantage of all the benefits a longer trip offers and make full use of the extra time you have.

For those who are interested in spending less time at the theme parks, there is plenty to do at Disney World. This includes taking in shows and parades, shopping for souvenirs, riding transportation around the resort, visiting Disney Springs, and more. If you are only going to be staying for a few days, you will likely have to cram all of your activities into a small amount of time. To ensure that you still balance fun and rest, plan on trying something new every day and use shorter trips to explore the entertainment options at each park.

Most people consider six to seven days to be ideal, whereas nine days or longer may be excessively beneficial unless your trip also includes activities that aren't found in theme parks. The main rule of thumb here is that the more days you take to go to Disney World, the more in-depth your activities will become. The pace of the trip may also become slower, which is okay, depending on what you are looking for. Worry less about getting everything done in a short amount of time and focus on enjoying yourself instead. As long as you break things up so that one day is not spent doing all of your activities, then you should be fine.

Regardless of your schedule, length of vacation, or where you are staying, you must remember that the tranquility of Disney World will be quickly disturbed if you do not make an effort to relax. There is no doubt that Disney World can be fun, exciting, and the most wonderful place on earth, but it's also important to remember that it's just a place. It's a lot like real life in the sense that there is no magic bullet or way to skip over the boring parts. The more effort you put into enjoying yourself at Disney World, the more you will enjoy yourself in the process.

Advance Dining Reservations

At Disney World, there are more than a hundred table-service restaurants spread across its four theme parks, Disney Springs, and numerous resort hotels. There is an abundance of cuisine, restaurant styles, and themes.

Booking Your Disney World Dining Reservations

Here is How You Reserve Online:

Install the FREE MyDisneyExperience mobile application. When you click the plus sign in a circle at the bottom of the screen, a list of options will appear. Select Check Dining Availability and enter the number of guests, date, and time. You can also choose "now" to see if any walk-up spots are available on the same day. You can also use the app to look for reservations based on experience, type of food, and location. Like on the website, you can reserve a table at a restaurant for the same day if available.

Here is How You Reserve Via Phone:

You should only make an ADR over the phone if you can't use the app or website or if you need to cancel a reservation less than two hours before it starts. You can make or cancel a reservation over the phone by calling 407-WDW-DINE and listening to the options.

Be sure to have a credit card handy prior to making dining reservations. Additionally, you can enter your credit card information in advance in your My Disney Experience account. If you do not show up or cancel within two hours of your reservation, Disney will charge you $10 per person.

Tips for Difficult-to-Reserve Advance Dining Reservations

For some, dining at Walt Disney World is a major event. Suppose you view your trip as a once-in-a-lifetime opportunity and want to go all out. Consider making reservations for a few table-service restaurants, at least one character dining experience, and possibly even a reservation at a tough-to-get-into restaurant for a romantic evening while the tadpoles are with a babysitter. If this describes you, you should make your reservations as soon as possible and consider staying on-site, particularly during peak times.

Even guests staying off-site can make dining reservations at Disney World. As opposed to certain perks that are exclusive to guests staying on-site at a Disney World hotel, ADRs are available to all guests, regardless of where they are staying (such as Early Theme Park Entry). However, valid theme park admission and a Disney Park Pass reservation are required at the dining location. Therefore, if you are dining at the Jungle Skipper Canteen, ensure that you have the appropriate tickets and park reservations to enter the Magic Kingdom on the date of your dining reservation.

The following are methods to maximize your chances of scoring the exact restaurants you want at precisely the right time:

1. The Refresh Method

If you tried to book an ADR and all (or most) of your choices are "unavailable," don't assume that they're completely gone, just that they're not available at the window you're in. Instead, use the My Disney Experience app or website to try again 10-15 minutes later. At some point during that time, a window opens up for you to select all your top choices.

This is because a dynamic system determines how likely you'll show up for your ADR and then places any "excess" dining slots into available windows as you refresh. It's not a completely exact science, but it DOES work. I've used this myself over the years and have gotten many extra restaurant options simply by refreshing my search on the app or website.

The possibility of getting your ADR timeslot using this method is random. It's not guaranteed, but it IS possible.

2. The Back-Up Plan Method

If you want to dine at a table-service restaurant is booked, don't despair. If you'd like to try another type of dining experience, especially those that are more likely to be available during your ADR window (such as table service restaurants within the theme parks), book an ADR for that restaurant using the "Check Availability" option on your My Disney Experience app or website and see if it pops up as available when you refresh. If not, move on to find another spot in the park since there are many restaurants that will be available at a kiosk or cart on Main Street USA, Fantasyland, or Liberty Square.

3. Change Your Party Size

Walt Disney World has concealed availability for smaller or odd-numbered groups since its reopening as part of its never-ending pursuit of yield management and revenue maximization. This is based on the theory that a party of one uses only half the capacity of a table for two and is statistically more likely to spend less. Due to the persistent imbalance between capacity and demand, Disney would prefer to turn away parties of one.

For parties with odd numbers, the solution is to look up your party's size and the table you'll be seated at. That is, a party of three should search for four, a party of five for six, and so on. You can change your reservation to reflect the precise number of guests attending your party during the mobile check-in process (or occasionally before). Just be sure to search for +1, your actual number; searching for anything higher (or lower) is a recipe for disaster.

The mobile check-in process has its limitations. Sometimes, you can increase your party size but keep it the same. This usually happens when a reservation window opens between 8 and 24 hours before your meal time. Also, if you're making a last-minute change after the dining window has closed, you need more time - so plan accordingly.

4. Multiple Devices, Computer Priority

Before your ADR window opens, you should log in to Disney's website and the "My Disney Experience" mobile app. All of this occurs at the crack of dawn, so there may be a strong inclination to complete it all in bed.

If you are truly committed, enable private browsing, login, and open a new tab for each restaurant you desire. From there, create your ADRs in ascending priority order. If something goes wrong, which it almost certainly will given that this is Disney IT, switch to the My Disney Experience app or a different device and carry on.

If you can't or don't want to log in two different times, complete your check-in window on the first device and then switch to the second, such as your smartphone or tablet's browser. Then pick up where you left off. If a table-service restaurant is not available when you resume the ADR search, refresh your search on the My Disney Experience app and continue.

5. Book for Off-Peak Times

The first thing to know about limited availability is that Disney keeps track of how many people are booking an ADR during a specific slot (usually 90 days out from arrival). This data is analyzed and used to determine how many tables can be made available at any given time — in theory, 50% for a "not so popular" time period like the early non-summer months, 70% if it's slightly busier, and 80% for a busy week in July or September.

The key is to book as much in advance as possible and to take advantage of the off-peak periods if they've opened up. The most popular timeframes are April, May, September, and October (along with November and a few weeks around Christmas). To get the maximum effect out of this strategy, you want to book your ADRs 30 days or more before these windows open up to the general public.

To do this, you should schedule your ADRs during many of this year's off-peak times but not all of them. Then, when they open up to the general public (and they will), you can book the remaining slots at that time. If you do so, you will have a well-rounded list of dining times, including the most popular periods, and can potentially secure reservations the day they open up. Guests who book during these peak times are less likely to be able to rebook at a later date, so if you last minute change your ADR time or restaurant, you're out.

6. Book 60 Days in Advance

Up to 60 days in advance, anyone can make an ADR for a table at a table service restaurant at Walt Disney World. On-site visitors can, however, make ADRs up to 60 days before the resort check-in date for the duration of their trip (up to 10 days). This makes it easier to make all of your ADRs all at once rather than day-by-day. The most foolproof and certain way to secure a reservation is to book 60 days prior to the start of your trip. This is technically a "soft" lock, so your dining times could likely change based on availability and the attrition of reservations on the day of your check-in. However, most people use this strategy, so incorporating it is a good idea.

Rather than hoping you don't run into any unexpected issues with your ADRs, you should have an entire itinerary planned out 60 days or more in advance and ready to execute at a moment's notice. This can be accomplished with a reservation that is split among multiple ADRs, allowing the most popular ones to open up while others are turned away. The advantage of this strategy is that you aren't locked into just one restaurant or one time period — if other times and restaurants are not available on the day you check in, you can move on to another category of interest.

However, if you are solely focused on the dining experience, you should book 60 days in advance. This will give Disney the most time possible to get a sense of how many people are looking at booking a particular restaurant in your party size and when they expect to arrive. If there is high demand for certain times and restaurants, it could open up availability earlier than anticipated.

7. Be Flexible and Play It By Ear

Sometimes, you may encounter a situation where the dining window has closed, or the restaurant is no longer available. The best thing to do when this happens is to move on to another one, but there are other tactics you can use.

Let's say you want to book a 7:00 reservation, but all of the slots between 6:00 and 9:00 are booked. You can start your search at 1:00 and then work your way up until that time frame opens up. Then search for the time period that includes that slot. If nothing is available there, go back to the previous time period, book it again, and then move on to the next one. Repeat until you find a time that opens up.

This strategy can also be used when the restaurant is unavailable, but you have another time that may open up. If you want to avoid booking an ADR that closes in 45 minutes, it's still possible to make it work by searching for the closest slot after 1:00 and then proceeding from there.

8. Use an Authorized Disney Vacation Planner

If you're intimidated by all of this or even if you understand it but still find it overwhelming, think about outsourcing your ADR creation. Many Authorized Disney Vacation Planners will make ADRs and assist with itineraries, which is one of the many benefits of using one. A travel agent with expertise in Disney vacations which has graduated from the company's school of knowledge is known as an Authorized Disney Vacation Planner.

Until recently, ADRs were an exclusively mouse-created experience. Disney eliminated the option of making them on your own or through an agency, so these planners are your only option. People who have used one say they're worth whatever they charge you (although there's no reason to pay more than $200) and save you time and stress — especially if this is your first time planning a trip.

If you feel like the timing of your vacation or other circumstances could be more predictable to figure out yourself, consider hiring a planner who specializes in Disney vacations. These agents can contact Disney on your behalf, booking all of the dining slots you desire even before they open up to the general public. In this way, you'll have the peace of mind that comes with booking early and will have a complete itinerary at your fingertips — all without the stress of figuring it out yourself.

As you can see, making ADRs can be complicated. It can be overwhelming if this is your first time planning a Disney vacation. However, even if you've made them before, it's never too late to improve on your strategy or even open up a new avenue of research. For most people, making ADRs is not a decision they make lightly but one that could easily change their entire trip experience.

Disney Genie and Disney Genie+

In place of FASTPASS, FastPass+, and Disney MaxPass, guests at Walt Disney World can now use Disney Genie and Disney Genie+, a paid version of the new free service. In addition, guests will have the option to pay additional fees for express access to select rides.

What is Disney Genie?

The "My Disney Experience" and Disneyland mobile applications now include a new, free planning tool. The new service aims to help guests have a more enjoyable experience in the parks by maximizing their time there. Using algorithms based on anticipated wait times, the Disney Genie technology helps you organize your park day according to your preferred schedule.

Before entering the park, you can log into the app and tell the Genie which rides, attractions, experiences, and meals you want, and the Genie (algorithm) will create a plan for you so that you spend less time in lines and more time enjoying the park. Like FASTPASS, Disney Genie discounts are based on the date and time of day. Nonetheless, regardless of which form of FASTPASS or Disney MaxPass you choose, you can use a FastPass+ to help create your Disney plans.

What is Disney Genie+?

Visitors can enter certain attractions without waiting in line by paying for an optional paid service that allows them to use the Lightning Lane entrance. Consider Lightning Lanes as the actual line you will wait in and Genie+ as the key that will grant you access to the line. Guests can choose 1 ride at a time and get different in-app experiences based on the park they are in. At Walt Disney World, a day pass costs between $15 and $29 per person, and guests have access to over 40 rides, but not all. Some attractions, like the Peoplemover at Magic Kingdom, need access to Lightning Lane. You can also use the app with augmented reality lenses and get special audio experiences in Walt Disney World theme parks.

You may choose your first Lightning Lane of the day at 7:00 a.m. from any of the available attractions. You can then continue adding Lightning Lanes throughout the day to minimize your wait time, but you can only reserve the Lightning Lane for each attraction once daily. When you use the Lightning Lane, you usually only have to wait 5–10 minutes. Compared to the standby line, where you have to wait at least 45 minutes, this saves a lot of time. Also, the number of guests seated on attractions is heavily skewed towards those using the Lightning Lane, so even if the wait time you see is 30 to 35 minutes or longer, the standby wait may still be in the 20 to 25-minute range. This is because the people in line for the ride themselves tend to be seated right away, and only guests waiting to enter through the Lightning Lane are running into longer waits.

You scan your MagicBand, Magic Mobile pass, or RFID card at the Lightning Lane entrance to redeem a reservation. This is what prevents guests from using the same reservation more than once.

Tips on Using Disney Genie+

1. Always Bring Your Phone

Because you can use Disney Genie+ on your mobile device, you should always bring the phone with you everywhere you go. You will also need a portable phone charger to get through the day at Disney World, but Genie+ will drain your battery even more. It is essential that you maintain a full charge throughout the day. With a fully charged phone (and, preferably, additionally charged phones among your party members), you will be able to book Lightning Lanes with Genie+ during practice. Technically, you can utilize the guest experience team, but doing so could be more efficient. That is why it is best to plan the day on your own.

2. Learn How to Book Your Next Lightning Lane.

You become eligible to reserve a new Lightning Lane when one of the following occurs:

- When you tap a Lightning Lane to redeem a reservation

- If you cancel your Lightning Lane reservation

- If your Lightning Lane reservation window of one hour expires

- If the ride for which you have a Lightning Lane reservation breaks down
- If two hours have passed since your last Lightning Lane reservation and no other qualifying events have occurred during that time

Each represents a time when you would expect Disney Genie+ to permit you to make a new Lightning Lane reservation. Remember that the ability to make a new Lightning Lane reservation becomes available after two hours of inactivity without qualifying events. However, this only applies once the theme park you have a reservation for has opened.

Therefore, if you book a Lightning Lane at 7:00 a.m. and have a reservation for Magic Kingdom on a day when the theme park opens at 8:00 a.m., you can book a new Lightning Lane at 10:00 a.m. if you're not doing anything and don't have any qualifying events during that time.

3. Reserve Lightning Lane for Popular Attractions

Prioritizing Lighting Lane reservations for high-demand attractions is important when using Disney Genie+. Lightning Lane reservations for multiple attractions typically sell out by the afternoon, even on low-crowd days. These attractions may need more Lightning Lane spots by lunchtime on moderate to heavy attendance days. Even before you are eligible to book a second Lightning Lane for the day, a couple may need more spots for you, leaving you with only the option to enter standby lines. Remember that Disney Genie+ can only make a reservation for one attraction at a time, so if you have all of your Lightning Lane reservations filled, there is nothing else you can do to shorten wait times on other rides.

The following are the attractions in each park where Lightning Lanes with Genie+ run out the quickest:

Animal Kingdom:
- Kilimanjaro Safaris
- Expedition Everest
- Na'vi River Journey

Epcot:
- Remy's Ratatouille Adventure
- Test Track
- Frozen Ever After

Hollywood Studios:

- Slinky Dog Dash

- Millennium Falcon: Smugglers' Run

Magic Kingdom:

- Jungle Cruise

- Peter Pan's Flight

There may be exceptions on a daily basis, but in general, the above attractions sell out the quickest. At Hollywood Studios, all attractions become scarce by midday (more on that later). As a general rule, your first Genie+ Lightning Lane selection for the day should be one of the attractions listed above.

4. Prioritize Ahead of Time

One underappreciated aspect of Disney Genie+ is the significance of time and speed at 7:00 a.m., particularly for the high-demand attractions discussed previously. Five seconds could be the difference between a 9:00 a.m. and 2:00 p.m. reservation for Lightning Lane at an attraction like Slinky Dog Dash. Therefore, you must prioritize the attractions your family wishes to ride and ensure that Disney Genie+ prioritizes those rides for you.

To accomplish this, you'll utilize the standard Disney Genie service (the app's free version). In the My Disney Experience app, select "My Day" followed by "Get Started Now" to access Disney Genie. Following that, you can choose the park where your day will begin. There, you can select up to eight attractions that you wish to ride.

At 7:00 a.m., you should only prioritize one or two attractions. The "Tip Board" section of the My Disney Experience app must be utilized in order to book Lightning Lane reservations. By prioritizing one or two attractions, you will ensure they appear at the top of your Tip Board, saving you precious seconds when booking them in the morning. You can always reselect attractions you are interested in by returning to the My Day section after receiving your first Lightning Lane or at any point during the day. But putting high-demand attractions at the top of your Tip Board for a 7 a.m. reservation will make a world of difference for your day.

5. Stack Multiple Lightning Lane Attractions

Simply put, Disney Genie+ doesn't care if your Lightning Lane reservations overlap, in contrast to its predecessor Fastpass+. Thus, you could have a Lightning Lane reservation for the 3:30–4:30 p.m. window and a second Lightning Lane reservation for the 3:40–

4:40 p.m. window; this does not result in a conflict or error in Disney Genie+ or the My Disney Experience app, other than a warning.

It allows you to manage your time more efficiently. Under the previous Fastpass system, visitors frequently waited an hour between attractions (or hit a standby line in between Fastpass attractions). Since Disney Genie+ allows you to schedule multiple rides within the same time frame, you can be more efficient in the parks. Taking a simple example, you could have a lengthy lunch and then complete three to four Lightning Lane reservations in one and a half hours.

In practice, you will likely stack Lightning Lane reservations without even realizing it. Remember to book new Lightning Lanes for each event that qualifies, or at least each time you access a new attraction or 120 minutes have passed. This will significantly assist you in optimizing your day with minimal effort.

6. Don't Cancel Lightning Lanes

The My Disney Experience app now allows users to modify Lightning Lane reservation times, which is an excellent update. This allows you to change your mind regarding a Lightning Lane reservation. You can reschedule it or select a different attraction altogether. Best of all, modifying Lightning Lanes does not reset the two-hour booking window for subsequent Lightning Lanes. This allows you to modify your Lightning Lanes without having to delay your next booking window.

To modify Lightning Lanes, go to your app's Tip Board or My Genie Day section and click the "modify plan" button. You can click the new attraction you want to visit after all attractions (including the one you booked) are displayed. Modify, rather than cancel, your Lightning Lanes; cancellation will reset your two-hour booking window.

7. Be Flexible

on very busy park days, return times can vary wildly and disappear in a matter of seconds. On days like these, it is recommended that you stick with the return times that Disney gives you. Lightning Lanes can now be modified to obtain better times, but there is no assurance that you will be able to do so. It's often not worth the stress, battery power, and time spent to try and modify your reservation.

By being flexible with your Lightning Lane reservations, you will have a much better experience. While some attractions have time-on-time-off, Lightning Lanes are often available all day. While this might mean you can pick up a quick return time for popular attractions, it's frequently not the case. Typically, large crowds are at the top attractions of each park, and those queues can often be eight to twelve minutes long.

With this in mind, you should pick your return times; an alternate plan can be to just come back while you are in the park (or eat dinner) and then return when you leave the park.

In addition, in the event that you choose to ride multiple attractions in a single trip, Lightning Lanes are often available throughout the day. The My Disney Experience app will offer a new Lightning Lane reservation opportunity every ten minutes or so. Attractions with longer wait times may offer several opportunities per hour. Accessing these opportunities during your morning or afternoon travel is far more efficient than waiting until you arrive back at your resort to get a new reservation.

You do not need Genie+ to enjoy the parks, and it provides a positive experience for you. It is just one of the many ways that guests can utilize their time. With that in mind, it's a tool worth implementing.

Maximizing Your Budget

It can be expensive to visit the Walt Disney World Resort. The costs can sometimes run into hundreds of dollars just for one day in the parks. For 2023, Walt Disney World ticket prices range from $109 to $189 per person. These ticket prices are for guests 10 and older. Guests aged 3 to 9 will pay slightly less, beginning at $104 per night. Guests under the age of three do not require a ticket. This does not include a 6.5% sales tax or additional expenses such as lodging, transportation, meals, and souvenirs.

The average cost of a trip to Disney World for a family of four is between $4,000 and $10,000, which is a considerable amount of money. A family of four can expect an average daily expense of $869, but there are ways to save money.

The following suggestions will help you maximize your budget while planning your Walt Disney World vacation:

1. Choose Dates Carefully

Similar to how airfare and hotel accommodations are more expensive on weekends and holidays, so are Disney World tickets. Ticket prices for Disney World now vary by date and park. Animal Kingdom is the least expensive Disney theme park, while Magic Kingdom costs the most. Individual tickets for a single day cost between $109 and $189. Depending on when they travel and which parks they visit, a family of four may incur additional daily ticket costs totaling $320. In addition, the cost of Disney Genie+, a pass that reduces wait times, varies by day. If you want to visit Disney World on a busy day, price differences can add up because it costs more (and sometimes even sells out) then.

Consider visiting Disney during the off-season, when the parks will be less crowded, and shorter wait times will allow you to see and do more. A benefit of visiting when it is less crowded? You can forego paying for Genie+ and decide whether Individual Lightning Lane access to attractions like Rise of the Resistance is worth the time saved.

Visit disneyworld.disneygo.com to view pass prices and make the necessary arrangements. If Disney World announces a promotion or discount, you may apply it retroactively to your existing reservation if it meets the terms of the offer. Discovering a deal and receiving an additional 10%-20% off your reservation is not unheard of.

2. Use Alternatives to Pay

You can easily save between 3 and 10% on the overall cost of your trip by purchasing discounted Disney gift cards to pay for everything, including your Disney hotel or Disney Vacation Club dues, park tickets, merchandise, and dining. You can purchase them from Target (with a RedCard for a 5% discount) or Sam's Club and BJ's for a 3% to 4%discount. If you buy Disney gift cards at grocery stores and office supply stores in a smart way, you can get bonus points on your rewards credit card even if you don't get a discount.

Wholesale warehouses are included in some cash-back credit cards' quarterly cash-back categories, increasing your savings. On occasion, chain stores such as Meijer, Kroger, and Lowe's offer additional discounts on gift cards so that you can save up to 10%. You can also redeem points for Disney World tickets or a hotel near Disney World, resulting in additional savings, depending on the credit cards in your wallet.

3. Eat at Lounges

The key to a successful Disney World vacation is striking a balance between maximizing park time and taking sufficient breaks to remind you that you're on vacation. Even though traditional table-service restaurants are typically expensive, a meal at Disney can be relaxing.

Visit one of the many atmospheric lounges at Disney World for lunch or dinner rather than eating every meal at a traditional full-service restaurant. You will still have a table and a server, but you will be able to order inexpensive lighter fare and inventive cocktails. The adult set lunch menu at Space 220 Restaurant in Epcot can cost up to $55 and the child set lunch menu can cost up to $29. However, you can still enjoy the view of the space from the lounge, which serves heavy appetizers for $12 to $18.

4. Stick To The Budget

You can choose which vacation activities you want to partake in and how much you can afford to spend on vacation by using the budgeting process. While it's difficult to stick to the budget when the world's most famous mouse is beckoning you outside your hotel room, try setting limits and self-regulating. For example, 50% of your trip is for entertainment (park tickets, restaurant meals, and character dining experiences) and 50% for transportation and lodging. No matter how hard it may be to limit yourself — especially if there are children involved — try to freeze your spending once that original budgeted amount has been spent.

If you go beyond your original plan, reward yourself with a day at the pool or a night out on the town. Doing so will ensure that you don't overspend and are still able to enjoy your vacation after it's over. Even though you may have to choose between spending time in a park and taking an afternoon nap, do what is best for you — after all, it's your vacation!

5. Bring Your Own Food

A significant way to save money is to bring your own groceries and food into the parks. Many people are shocked by this simple Disney World money-saving tip. They think Disney World is like a movie theater with a "No Food Allowed" policy. Actually, they would be wrong. Disney permits guests to bring food into the parks. You can bring in soft-sided coolers with food and drinks. You can also bring a small backpack to store your food and drinks. The only rule is that Disney does not allow alcohol or glass containers into the park.

If you're bringing your own food into the park, consider eating at one of the quick-service restaurants with tables. You'll bypass much of the time spent waiting in line at a table-service restaurant, and you can eat throughout your vacation schedule. Consider grabbing a quick breakfast or lunch at a counter-service location, but only if it's something you plan to eat many times during your trip. In this situation, it may be less expensive to pay admission to a theme park and dine there.

There are numerous ways to maximize the budget for your Disney World vacation. There are also ways to completely reduce your expenses. There are also ways to minimize your expenses completely. Your options will depend on your money management skills and how much you are willing to compromise on the number of attractions and rides you can enjoy at the theme parks. Still, it's possible to enjoy Disney World for a fraction of the cost by juggling these techniques appropriately.

Choosing a Walt Disney World Resort to stay in can be challenging. It's great to have options, but your choice of hotel or resort will ultimately depend on personal preference, the number of travelers in your party, and your budget.

Overview of Disney-Owned Options

The following are a few of the numerous options available at Walt Disney World, ranging from Value to Deluxe:

Value Disney World Hotels

Disney's All-Star Movies Resort

Image: Michael Rivera

Disney Resort that is inexpensive for guests who value their money. Decorations honoring Fantasia, 101 Dalmatians, Toy Story, The Mighty Ducks, and The Love Bug abound in Disney magic. There are either two double beds or one king-sized bed in each room. Please note that rooms with king beds are accessible for wheelchairs. Although they can be requested, guests with special needs are given priority.

Each room contains a beverage cooler, a nightstand, a telephone, a small table with two chairs, an armoire, a television, a wall mirror, an alarm clock, and an open closet space with additional shelving. The shower area is enclosed by tiles depicting film reels and shower curtains adorned with stars. In keeping with the movie motif, the light fixtures are shaped like popcorn boxes and stars. In the closet is a small key-operated wall safe. Each room is equipped with central air conditioning—guests who require Internet access while on vacation will have access to complimentary WiFi.

Location:

1991 W. Buena Vista Drive, Lake Buena Vista, FL 32830

Phone:

(407) 939-7000

Maximum Persons Per Room:

4

Room Rates:

- For Standard Room - Ranges from $128 to $289 depending on the season.

- For Preferred Room - Ranges from $155 to $323 depending on the season.

Tip:

The "preferred" and more expensive sections are Fantasia, Toy Story, and 101 Dalmatians. Those desiring a quieter, lower-traffic area should request the Love Bug buildings. Guests staying in the Mighty Ducks buildings may find it more convenient to catch the bus in front of Melody Hall at the All-Star Music Resort.

Disney's All-Star Music Resort

An ideal option for budget-conscious Disney World visitors. Its whimsical design features oversized musical icons representing Jazz, Rock, Calypso, Broadway, and Country music.

The rooms at Disney's All-Star Music Resort are furnished with two double beds, a beverage cooler, a small table with two chairs, a small safe with a key, a television, a dresser, and an alarm clock. Separate from the bathtub and toilet is a vanity area containing a single sink and mirror. There are also rooms with king-size beds available. These are handicap-accessible rooms and therefore have larger bathrooms with no tub but a wheelchair-accessible shower instead.

Family Suites feature two rooms that can accommodate up to six guests. The Master bedroom features a queen-sized bed, a desk, and a television.

Suites at the All-Star Resort feature a kitchenette equipped with a refrigerator, microwave, sink, and coffeemaker. Two full bathrooms with separate vanities are available.

Location:

1801 W. Buena Vista Drive, Lake Buena Vista, FL

Phone:

(407) 939-6000

Maximum Per Room:

2-6

Room Rates:

- Standard Room - Ranges from $128 to $289, depending on the season.

- Preferred Room - Ranges from $167 to $329, depending on the season.

- Family Suites - Ranges from $323 to $658 depending on the season

Tip:

Choose the Jazz Inn for a room in a quieter area close to the food court and bus stop.

Disney's All-Star Sports Resort

Image: Michael Rivera

A sports-themed resort featuring an abundance of sports memorabilia throughout the property. It's also home to the ESPN Wide World of Sports Complex, which features a 150-meter competition swimming pool and soccer, hockey, and baseball fields. There's a basketball court, batting cages, and a bocce court.

The rooms are slightly more compact than those at moderate resorts (260 square feet as opposed to 314 square feet). A standard room includes two double beds (or one king-sized bed), a beverage cooler, a small table with two chairs, a television, nightstand, telephone, dresser, wall mirror, luggage rack, closet space, themed light fixtures (megaphones or stars), and an alarm clock radio. Separate from the bathtub and toilet is a vanity area containing a single sink and mirror. In the closet is a small, key-operated wall safe for storing your valuables. Guests who require Internet access while on vacation will have access to complimentary WiFi.

There are also rooms with king-sized beds, but these are the handicapped-accessible rooms with larger bathrooms and a roll-in shower instead of a bathtub. All of the rooms have central air conditioning.

Location:

1701 West Buena Vista Drive, Lake Buena Vista, FL 32830

Phone:

(407) 407-5000

Maximum Persons Per Room:

4

Room Rates:

- For Standard Room - Ranges from $128 to $289 depending on the season.

- For Preferred Room - Ranges from $160 to $321 depending on the season.

Tip:

Guests must bring towels from their rooms to use at the pool and contact housekeeping to request additional towels for their rooms. Life jackets are provided for free and can be obtained from the pool area. Check the lifeguard stands' backs for park hours and weather information.

Disney's Art of Animation Resort

Themed after well-known Disney animated classics like Finding Nemo, Cars, The Little Mermaid, and The Lion King, this resort primarily provides family suites. The rooms feature age-appropriate decor inspired by these films.

Disney's Art of Animation Resort rooms varies depending on the building's theme.

The Finding Nemo rooms feature coral-shaped chairs and bubble-shaped ceiling lights. The bathroom is designed to resemble the submarine scene from the film, right down to the porthole mirror. Fans of The Lion King will enjoy seeing Zazu on the headboards and Pumbaa and Timon on the shower curtain. The Cars suites are located within the "Cozy Cone Motel," and the room's decor definitely evokes a "motel" atmosphere. A map of Radiator Springs adorns the top of the coffee table, which features tool chests as drawers and storage areas.

Location:

1850 Animation Way, Lake Buena Vista, FL 32821

Phone:

(407) 938-7000

Maximum Per Room:

4 - 6

Room Rates:

- The Little Mermaid Standard Room - Ranges from $201 to $392, depending on the season.

- Family Suites - Ranges from $459 to $839 depending on the season

- Cars or Lion King Family Suites - Ranges from $475 to $845 depending on the season

- Finding Nemo Family Suites - Ranges from $502 to $912 depending on the season

Tips:

Bring your own linens. Towels are provided for the pools, but there is no housekeeping available. The rooms with balconies require a Disney Vacation Club (DVC) membership to use the balcony.

Disney's Pop Century Resort

Value-minded destination for guests wanting Disney magic on a budget. You're transported back in time as you find yourself surrounded by oversized icons paying homage to the 20th Century.

The rooms at Pop Century are comparable to those at Disney's other value resorts. Standard rooms are 260 square feet in size and feature either one Queen-size bed plus one Queen-size pull-down bed or one King-size bed. Preferred rooms are available for an additional fee and are located closer to Classic Hall.

Location:

1050 Century Dr, Lake Buena Vista, FL 32830

Phone:

(407) 938-4000

Maximum Persons Per Room:

4

Room Rates:

- Standard Room - Ranges from $174 to $367 depending on the season

- Standard Pool View - Ranges from $182 to $381 depending on the season

- Preferred Room - Ranges from $194 to $393 depending on the season

- Preferred Pool View - Ranges from $205 to $403 depending on the season

Tips:

Guests must bring towels from their rooms to use at the pool and contact housekeeping to request additional towels for their rooms. Life jackets are provided for free and can be obtained from the pool area. Check the lifeguard stands' backs for park hours and weather information.

Disney's Fort Wilderness Resort & Campground

These cabins are an excellent option for those in search of a more rustic log cabin dwelling. Camping in an RV or a tent is permitted at the campgrounds.

Each cabin has a separate bedroom with a double bed, bunk beds, and a pull-down bed in the living area. The cabins will sleep 6 people. There is a full bathroom, hairdryer, and living/dining area. This area has a sofa and cable TV. The dining area has seating for 6. You'll also be provided with an iron/ironing board. The kitchen has all major appliances minus the food. A small deck with your charcoal grill and picnic table is outside each cabin. There is parking for one car at your cabin. The cabins have free wireless internet access.

The lush wilderness provides privacy for the 847 campsites throughout the 21 loops. The sites are approximately 25' wide and range from 25' to 65' in length. They are a combination of paved driveway and sandy pad. All sites have running water, electricity, WiFi, cable TV hookups, charcoal grills, and picnic tables. There are full hook-up sites that provide sanitary disposal.

Location:

4510 N. Fort Wilderness Trail, Lake Buena Vista, FL 32830

Phone:

(407) 824-2900

Maximum Persons Per Room:

4 - 6

Rates:

- Campsites: From $75 - $189 per night
- Cabins: From $364-568 per night

Tip:

Comfort stations with air conditioning are located throughout the resort. Restrooms, private showers, laundry facilities, an ice maker, and telephones are available. Guests can use their MagicBands to access laundromats that are open around the clock. Rentable camping equipment is available for those in need. Pets are permitted in designated areas and can be boarded at a kennel near the resort's entrance. Check-in begins at 1 p.m. and ends at 11 a.m. Guests checking into the campgrounds may register at the Reception Outpost's drive-through windows.

Moderate Disney World Hotels

Disney's Caribbean Beach Resort

Moderate-priced A resort is ideal for vacationers seeking value and amenities that will enhance their stay. Surrounded by a 45-acre lake, the resort's "island theme" is reflected in its tropical décor, white sand beaches, and seven inviting pools.

At 300 square feet, the rooms are slightly smaller than those at other Disney resorts. Some rooms offer a pull-down Murphy bed to accommodate a fifth guest in addition to the standard two Queen beds. There is a flat-screen television in each room. In-room amenities include a mini-fridge, an iron and ironing board, and a single-cup coffeemaker. The room safe in these accommodations can accommodate a 15-inch laptop. Two sink basins are located outside the shower/toilet, allowing one person to get ready while another shower. In standard rooms, a sliding barn-style door separates this area from the sleeping area; in Pirate-themed rooms, a curtain is used.

Location:

1300 Old West Works, Lake Buena Vista, FL 32830

Phone:

(407) 938-2101

Maximum Persons Per Room:

2- 4

Room Rates:

- Standard View - Ranges from $258 to $479 per night, depending on the season

- Standard View – 5th Sleeper - Ranges from $277 to $494 per night, depending on the season.

- Water or Pool View - Ranges from $296 to $514 per night, depending on the season

- King Bed - Ranges from $303 to $523 per night, depending on the season

- Water or Pool View – 5th Sleeper - Ranges from $313 to $529 per night, depending on the season

- Preferred Room - Ranges from $496 to $551 per night, depending on the season

Tip:

A limited supply of pull-out sofabeds can be rented for an additional $18 per night. The resort has a "no check-in" policy, meaning that guests must register at the lobby's front desk upon arrival.

Disney's Port Orleans Resort - French Quarter

Ideal for guests with a moderate budget who desire a unique resort experience. The theme is Mardi Gras in New Orleans. With an abundance of intricate ironwork and flowering gardens, romance and excitement are in the air. The main pool at Doubloon Lagoon includes a dragon slide and alligator fountains. Port Orleans guests have access to Riverside's amenities as well.

The rooms are decorated with warm hues that evoke the spirit of New Orleans. Bedspreads in purple and gold with the Fleur de Lis motif, gold curtains, and dark wood accents. The 314-square-foot rooms feature two sink basins outside the bathroom so that one guest can get ready while another shower. The rooms feature two queen beds. All Disney moderate resorts feature H20 bath products in the rooms (shampoo, conditioner, and soaps). The upgraded version of the product is sold in the gift shop adjacent to the lobby at Jackson Square. The rooms have flat-screen televisions with easy access to HDMI ports and audio and video inputs. This is convenient if you bring video game systems for your children or if you want to connect your camcorder to review your vacation footage.

Some rooms are available with a king-size bed, and some are handicapped-accessible with a wheelchair-accessible shower in place of a tub.

Location:

2201 Orleans Drive, Lake Buena Vista, FL 32830

Phone:

(407) 934-5353

Fax:

(407) 934-5353

Maximum Persons Per Room:

2 - 4

Room Rates:

- Standard View – Ranges from $278 to $451 per night, depending on the season

- Garden View – Ranges from $287 to $486 per night, depending on the season

- River View – Ranges from $303 to $497 per night, depending on the season

- Pool View – Ranges from $303 to $505 per night, depending on the season

- King Bed – Ranges from $315 to $523 per night, depending on the season

Tip:

Request Buildings 1 or 6 for a room with a peaceful river view.

Disney's Coronado Springs Resort

Image: Michiel1972

This destination is ideal for guests with a moderate budget who desire a resort experience. Its three Southwest-themed sections encompass a 15-acre lake. With a 46-

foot-tall pyramid and cascading waterfall, the main pool with an Aztec theme is one of Disney's best.

The rooms at Coronado Springs are among the nicest of moderate resorts, having been renovated in 2009. The average guestroom is 314 square feet and contains two queen beds (or one king-sized bed). In addition, the room features a table with two chairs, a wall mirror, a coffeemaker (with complimentary coffee), an iron and ironing board, a television, a dresser, a nightstand, a hair dryer, a ceiling fan, a single sink and mirror in a vanity area outside the bathtub and toilet. There is a small wall safe for valuables in the closet. Coronado Springs offers complimentary WiFi in all of its rooms. There are also handicap-accessible rooms with a king-size bed and a roll-in shower instead of a bathtub.

Location:

1000 West Buena Vista Drive, Lake Buena Vista, FL 32830

Phone:

(407) 939-1000

Fax:

(407) 939-1001

Maximum Persons Per Room:

- Standard View - 4

- King - 2

- Water View - 4

- Junior Suite - 6

- Junior Suite - King - 4

- Casitas 1-Bedroom Suite - 6

- 1-Bedroom Suite - Sleeps 4

- Casitas Executive Suite - Sleeps 6

Room Rates:

- Standard View - Ranges from $250 to $446 per night, depending on the season

- Water View - Ranges from $298 to $492 per night, depending on the season

- King Bed - Ranges from $338 to $497 per night, depending on the season

- Preferred Room - Ranges from $340 to $504 per night, depending on the season
- Preferred Room – King - Ranges from $345 to $511 per night depending on the season
- 'Tower – Standard View - Ranges from $303 to $602 per night depending on the season
- Water View – King - Ranges from $353 to $557 per night, depending on the season
- Tower – Water View - Ranges from $352 to $605 per night, depending on the season
- Tower – Standard View – King Bed - Ranges from $387 to $608 per night, depending on the season
- Tower – Water View – King Bed - Ranges from $413 to $627 per night, depending on the season
- Tower – Standard View – Club Access - Ranges from $428 to $975 per night depending on the season
- Tower – Deluxe Suite – Club Access - Ranges from $672 to $1322 per night, depending on the season
- Casitas – 1 Bedroom Suite - Ranges from $1043 to $1572 per night depending on the season
- 1 Bedroom Suite – King - Ranges from $1050 to $1577 per night depending on the season
- Tower – One Bedroom Suite – Club Access - Ranges from $1236 to $1875 per night depending on the season
- Casitas – Executive Suite - Ranges from $1473 to $2259 per night depending on the season
- Tower – Presidential Suite – Club Access - Ranges from $1732 to $3520 per night, depending on the season

Tip:

In addition to swimming, there is much to do at Disney's Coronado Springs. There are two arcades, the Jumping Beans Arcade in El Centro adjacent to Panchito's and the Iguana Arcade at the main pool area of the Dig Site. Standard, tandem, and Surrey bicycles are available for rent to cyclists who wish to tour the 0.9-mile-long Esplanade that encircles Lago Dorado.

This moderately priced resort is brimming with southern charm. While enjoying the "Old Man Island" swimming complex, you will be surrounded by stately mansions and beautiful gardens.

Port Orleans Riverside is the most luxurious and comfortable moderate resort operated by Disney. The muted hues of moss green and wedgewood blue provide an excellent contrast to the headboards made of dark wood that depict scenes from the resort. Each room has two queen-sized beds that make for a restful night's sleep, especially after a long day exploring the theme parks. All Disney moderate resorts feature H2O bath products in the rooms (shampoo, conditioner, and soaps). In the gift shop, an upgraded version of the H2O product is available. The rooms feature flat-screen televisions with audio and video inputs, as well as complimentary WiFi. There is a mini-fridge, wall safe (not large enough for a laptop), coffee maker, iron and ironing board, and hair dryer in each room.

The Mansion rooms are themed as Royal guest rooms and feature extra touches such as custom drapes, ornately decorated beds, and fiber optic-lit headboards that create a personal "fireworks" display above each bed.

Location:

1251 Riverside Drive, Lake Buena Vista, FL 32830

Phone:

(407) 934-6000

Fax:

(407) 934-5777

Maximum Persons Per Room:

4

Room Rates:

- Standard View - Ranges from $278 to $451 per night, depending on the season

- Woods View - Ranges from $291 to $475 per night, depending on the season

- Standard View – 5th Sleeper - Ranges from $294 to $478 per night, depending on the season

- Woods View – 5th Sleeper - Ranges from $309 to $489 per night, depending on the season

- Pool View - Ranges from $299 to $480 per night, depending on the season

- King Bed - Ranges from $338 to $497 per night, depending on the season

- Preferred Room - Ranges from $340 to $519 per night, depending on the season

- River View - Ranges from $340 to $519 per night, depending on the season

- Royal Guest Room – Standard View - Ranges from $340 to $524 per night, depending on the season

- Royal Guest Room – Woods View - Ranges from $346 to $532 per night, depending on the season

- Royal Guest Room – River View - Ranges from $353 to $555 per night, depending on the season

Tip:

From 4 p.m. until midnight, room service is restricted to pizza, salads, soft drinks, and beer.

Deluxe Disney World Resort Hotels
Animal Kingdom Lodge

Image: D. Sikes (alaskanent)

The Animal Kingdom Lodge offers a truly unique Deluxe resort experience that is unforgettable. You are in the middle of an African wildlife preserve surrounded by free-roaming animals that approach the resort in awe-inspiring proximity. This resort features a variety of restaurants, a health club with spa services, and a zero-entry pool with an attractive theme.

Two queen beds (one queen bed with bunkbeds or a king bed with a daybed are also available), a television, a refrigerator, a table with two chairs, a closet, and a vanity area separate from the bathtub and commode are standard room amenities. Details that make this a deluxe resort became apparent upon closer inspection: ornate wood-carved furniture, two under-mounted sinks in the vanity with a marble countertop and contemporary fixtures, and an LCD HDTV with a separate box to plug in your own devices. Each room features a private balcony. The rooms with the Savanna View feature views of the 33-acre wildlife preserve.

In addition to guest suites and concierge-level accommodations, Disney's Animal Kingdom Lodge features guest suites. The Concierge-level accommodations provide access to the Kilimanjaro Club lounge, bathrobes, turndown service, and the opportunity to participate in two exclusive safari activities (for an additional fee.)

This is a Disney Deluxe Resort with all the amenities you would expect from a resort of this caliber. The hotel offers valet or self-parking, room service, bell staff, and a concierge desk to its guests.

Location:

2901 Osceola Parkway, Lake Buena Vista, FL 32830

Phone:

(407) 938-3000

Room Rates:

- Standard View - Ranges from $469 to $842 per night, depending on the season
- Standard View – King Bed - Ranges from $486 to $861 per night, depending on the season
- Pool View - - Ranges from $506 to $884 per night, depending on the season
- Pool View – King Bed - Ranges from $903 to $555 per night, depending on the season
- Savanna View - Ranges from $672 to $1113 per night, depending on the season
- Savanna View – King Bed - Ranges from $691 to $1132 per night, depending on the season

Tip:

Special requests should be made during the reservation process (such as a preferred room view), but you should be aware that these cannot be guaranteed.

This luxurious Walt Disney World resort can be found on the 25-acre Crescent Lake. Its pastel hues and beachfront atmosphere are indicative of its New England seaside motif. It is most well-known for its three-acre Stormalong Bay pool complex, which features a 150-foot slide and sandy bottom. This resort is conveniently located within walking distance of Epcot and features a variety of dining and recreation options.

With their aquatic color palette and glossy finishes, these rooms are inspired by the ocean. The mother-of-pearl and dark wood frames of the powder blue upholstered headboards are outlined with mother-of-pearl. Blue-green and silver accents create a sophisticated and airy environment. There are French doors leading from each room to a patio or balcony.

Beach Club standard rooms offer a variety of view options, all of which affect the room rate. Standard view rooms overlook the rooftop or parking lot, Garden view rooms overlook the resort's numerous courtyards, and water view rooms overlook Crescent Lake or Stormalong Bay (the resort's primary pool). Each room features an alarm clock with an MP3 player, a mini refrigerator, a ceiling fan, a coffee maker with a tea and coffee setup, a hair dryer, an ice bucket, a safe, an iron and ironing board, pool towels, a desk and chair, a telephone, and a television.

Location:

1800 Epcot Resorts Blvd, Lake Buena Vista, FL 32830

Phone:

(407) 934-8000

Maximum Occupancy:

5

Room Rates:

- Standard View - Ranges from $543 to $982 per night, depending on the season

- King Bed - Ranges from $549 to $988 per night, depending on the season

- Garden or Woods View - Ranges from $592 to $1,048 per night, depending on the season

- Water View - Ranges from $699 to $1,113 per night, depending on the season

- Deluxe Room - Ranges from $756 to $1,186 per night, depending on the season

Tip:

The Disney's Beach Club club level provides access to the Stone Harbor Club (concierge lounge). The lounge offers a continental breakfast in the morning, afternoon snacks, and hot and cold hors d'oeuvres in the evening. Additionally, dessert and alcohol are served later in the evening. Throughout the day, two concierge cast members are available to assist guests with priority seating arrangements, Lightning Lane scheduling, and a variety of other services.

Disney's Boardwalk Inn

Image: traveljunction

This Deluxe seaside-themed resort on the shores of Crescent Lake evokes images of a bygone era. Evenings in the entertainment district, which is fronted by a traditional wooden boardwalk, are filled with nonstop fun. With restaurants, clubs, shops, and traditional carnival games, this location is ideal for vacationers looking to spice up their trip. You will be able to walk to both Epcot and Disney's Hollywood Studios.

The average guest room is approximately 370 square feet in size and is furnished with two queen-sized beds (or one king-sized bed), a daybed, an armoire, a television, a nightstand, a refrigerator, a small table with two chairs, a wall mirror, a small key-locked wall safe, a telephone, and a separate double vanity and mirror for the bathtub and commode.

The bathrooms and double vanities are constructed from marble. Some rooms with a king-size bed may be wheelchair-accessible, with a roll-in shower in place of a bathtub. In addition, each room features an iron, ironing board, Pack-n-Play crib, hair dryer, and vanity mirror. Guests who need to connect to their home or office via the Internet while on vacation will have access to high-speed Internet.

The rooms at The Boardwalk Inn are comprised of dark woods, contrasting patterns of stripes and toile, and a combination of jewel tones and lighter hues. With views overlooking gardens, pools, or the boardwalk itself, it achieves a sense of relaxed elegance and fun.

Location:

2101 N Epcot Resorts Blvd, Lake Buena Vista, FL 32830

Phone:

(407) 939-6200

Maximum Persons Per Room:

4

Room Rates:

- Standard View - Ranges from $597 to $1,044 per night, depending on the season
- Garden View - Ranges from $626 to $1,065 per night, depending on the season
- Water View - Ranges from $747 to $1,136 per night, depending on the season

Tip:

24-hour room service is available daily. Choose from an assortment of American classics in addition to resort-specific specialties. Press "Dining Options" on your in-room phone to place an order. All delivery orders will be subject to an 18% gratuity, a $3.00 delivery fee, and a 6.5% sales tax. Possible minimum order quantity.

Disney's Contemporary Resort

At Disney's Contemporary Resort, standard rooms and suites are available. These rooms are among the largest on Disney property at 422 square feet.

Patios on the first floor of rooms in the Garden wings are shared with neighbors. Guests who need to connect to their home or office via the Internet while on vacation will have access to a high-speed connection.

There are 25 suites with views of the park or the lake. There are available one- and two-bedroom suites with two queen-size beds and sleeper sofas. Suites are furnished with two-line speakerphones, an additional phone in the bathroom, a hair dryer, a bathrobe, and a turndown service.

The eleven Concierge suites are located on floors 12 and 14. A lounge offering a continental breakfast, daily appetizers, an evening cheese bar, desserts, cordials, free beer, wine, soft drinks, and bottled water; and concierge services that include making dinner and recreation reservations, answering questions, and planning excursions.

Location:

4600 North World Drive, Lake Buena Vista, FL 32830

Phone:

(407) 824-1000

Maximum Persons Per Room:

2-4

Room Rates:

- Garden Wing – Standard View - Ranges from $550to $988 per night, depending on the season

- Garden Wing – Garden View - Ranges from $557 to $1,074 per night, depending on the season

- Garden Wing – King - Ranges from $656 to $1,080 per night, depending on the season

- Garden Wing – Deluxe Room - Ranges from $663 to $1,127 per night, depending on the season

- Main Tower – Lake View - Ranges from $774 to $1,216 per night, depending on the season.

- Main Tower – Theme Park View - Ranges from $870 to $1,348 per night, depending on the season.

Tip:

The rooms in the south wing are closer to the hotel's pool and convention center. The rooms in the Tower offer breathtaking views of Bay Lake, the Seven Seas Lagoon, and Magic Kingdom Park. They are also near the monorail station, restaurants, and stores. The monorail may be quite distant from the Garden wing rooms. Due to the proximity of the Tower to the Grand Canyon Concourse, however, some rooms may need to be quieter.

Image: Sixflashphoto

The finest deluxe resort by Disney has everything. The hotel exudes opulence, from its opulent design to its elegantly appointed guestrooms. From gourmet dining to a full-service spa, the hotel can accommodate your every whim. There are numerous options for recreation, including swimming complexes with the ideal Magic Kingdom backdrop. Even though you won't want to leave, the monorail will transport you to the parks when you're ready.

A standard guestroom accommodates five people, but the Lodge Tower and Concierge Deluxe rooms accommodate four. The Grand Floridian's dormer or "attic" rooms are located on the upper floors beneath the gabled roofs. These rooms are slightly smaller than the Standard rooms, but the vaulted ceilings make them appear larger. A private balcony makes up for the small size of the room. Dormer rooms sleep 4 adults.

Club-level rooms include club concierge desk services, access to the concierge lounge, complimentary DVD rentals from the resort, complimentary bathrobes, turn-down service, and alcoholic beverages from 7 a.m. to 10 p.m. upon request.

Location:

4401 Floridian Way, Lake Buena Vista, FL 32830-1000

Phone:

(407) 824-3000

Maximum Persons Per Room:

2-8

Room Rates:

- Garden Wing – Standard View - Ranges from $550 to $988 per night, depending on the season

- Garden Wing – Garden View - Ranges from $557 to $1,074 per night, depending on the season

- Garden Wing – King - Ranges from $656 to $1,080 per night, depending on the season

- Garden Wing – Deluxe Room - Ranges from $663 to $1,127 per night, depending on the season

- Main Tower – Lake View - Ranges from $774 to $1,216 per night, depending on the season.

- Main Tower – Theme Park View - Ranges from $870 to $1,348 per night, depending on the season.

- Standard Room – Atrium Club Level - Ranges from $1,000 to $1,552 per night, depending on the season.

- Standard Room – King – Club Level - Ranges from $1,006 to $1,619 per night, depending on the season.

- Theme Park View – Atrium Club Level - Ranges from $1,059 to $1,797 per night, depending on the season.

- Garden Wing – 1 Bedroom Suite Access - Ranges from $2,360 to $2,670 per night, depending on the season

- Garden Wing -1 Bedroom Hospitality Ste Access - Ranges from $2,845 to $1,619 per night, depending on the season

- Bay Lake View – 1 Bedroom Suite – Club Level - Ranges from $2,999 to $3,275 per night, depending on the season

- Theme Park View 1 Bedroom Suite – Club Level - Ranges from $2,013 to $3,674 per night, depending on the season.

- Bay Lake View – 2 Bedroom Suite – Club Level - Ranges from $2,770 to $5,114 per night, depending on the season

- Theme Park View 2 Bedroom Suite – Club Level - Ranges from $2,890 to $5,231 per night, depending on the season.

- Theme Park View Presidential Suite Club Level - Ranges from $3,277 to $5,594 per night, depending on the season.

Tip:

Be certain to examine the walls behind the front desk. There you will find stacks of the original metal keys used at the resort before the switch to personalized key cards.

Walt Disney World Swan and Dolphin Resorts

These luxurious resorts are located near EPCOT, Disney's Hollywood Studios, and the Boardwalk's entertainment district. These resorts are situated on Crescent Lake and offer spacious guest rooms, a variety of dining options, and a three-acre pool complex with hot tubs and a waterfall-adorned grotto.

The Disney Dolphin Hotel is closest to the Yacht Club and Beach Club Resorts, while the Disney Swan Hotel is closest to the Boardwalk Resort area. Guests staying at the Swan and Dolphin resorts enjoy many of the same perks as those staying at a Disney World resort and looking to avoid crowds. Then take advantage of the exclusive Early Entry offered by Disney. The transportation to Disney's theme parks, water parks, and Disney Springs is satisfactory. Everything is included and complimentary with your stay.

Whether you select the Swan or the Dolphin, you'll experience the best of both worlds. The recreation, dining, and entertainment venues are accessible to all guests. These properties are resorts in every sense of the term. It is rare for a destination to render theme parks secondary. This is what you can expect when staying at Walt Disney World's Swan and Dolphin resorts.

Location:

Lake Buena Vista, FL 32830.

Phone:

1-800-227-1500

For the Dolphin (407) 934-4000

For the Swan: (407) 934-3000

Maximum Persons Per Room:

5

Room Rates:

- Standard View - Ranges from $336 to $1,075 per night, depending on the season

- Lake View - Ranges from $436 to $1,242 per night, depending on the season

- Resort View Without Balcony - Ranges from $436 to $1,242 per night, depending on the season

- Resort View With Balcony - Ranges from $710 to $1,368 per night, depending on the season

- Club Level Suite - Ranges from $1,751 to $1,957 per night, depending on the season

- Presidential Suite - Ranges from $3,882 to $4,383 per night, depending on the season

Tip:

The Swan and Dolphin at Walt Disney World offer a bus service. Buses depart approximately every 15 to 20 minutes.

Disney's Polynesian Village Resort

Image: Lexi Scott (lxsscott)

This deluxe resort is located across from the Magic Kingdom on the shores of the Seven Seas Lagoon. Its South Seas location is ideal for guests seeking a genuine tropical experience. There is a pool with a volcano theme, watercraft rentals, and a wonderful selection of restaurants and shops. The hotel's proximity to the monorail makes transportation simple.

The recently renovated rooms at the Polynesian have a Moana motif. There are several characters from the film scattered throughout the area. View options for standard rooms at the Polynesian include a garden view, lagoon view, and theme park view. Two queen beds and a day bed are found in rooms with a lagoon or theme park view. Rooms with a view of the Garden feature only two queen beds.

The majority of suites include a kitchenette and a living area. In addition, they provide 2 queen-size beds, 1 king-size bed, and possibly 2 Sico beds (that pull out from the wall). The bathrooms feature beautiful marble tubs. In keeping with the South Seas motif, the furniture is made of bamboo and cane with stone table tops. Suite amenities also include speakerphones with a second line, bathrobes, an iron and ironing board, Polynesian-themed stationery, and a nightly turndown service. These amenities are offered in the standard concierge rooms as well.

Location:

1600 Seven Seas Drive, Bay Lake, FL 32830-1000

Phone:

(407) 824-2000

Maximum Persons Per Room:

4-5

Room Rates:

- Standard View - Ranges from $662 to $1,184 per night, depending on the season

- Pool or Marina View - Ranges from $757 to $1,249 per night, depending on the season

- Lagoon View - Ranges from $835 to $1,438 per night, depending on the season

- Garden View – Club Level - Ranges from $904 to $1,500 per night, depending on the season

- Theme Park View - Ranges from $1,088 to $1,550 per night, depending on the season

Tip:

24-hour room service is available daily. Salads, hot sandwiches, appetizers, and burgers are available from 11:30 a.m. to midnight. From 5 p.m. to 10:30 p.m., the restaurant serves appetizers, barbecued ribs, sweet-and-sour chicken, shrimp and pasta, pork tenderloin, filet mignon, steak, and desserts.

Star Wars: Galactic Starcruiser Resort Hotel

The Star Wars: Galactic Starcruiser is a fully immersive hotel experience in which visitors will "Immediately become a galactic citizen and experience all that entails, including donning the appropriate attire. Once you leave Earth, you'll discover a starship teeming with characters, stories, and adventures. It is 100 percent immersive, and the story will permeate every moment of your day, culminating in a unique journey for each visitor."

Each Standard Cabin is outfitted with comfort-enhancing furnishings and fixtures, such as a pullout table, a television with entertainment from your home planet, and a window with a view of space.

One-bedroom Galaxy Class Suites feature a living area with a built-in seating area and all the amenities of Standard Cabins, plus a double vanity bathroom, bar area, two windows with views of space, and a few Star Wars extras.

Grand Captain's Suites with two bedrooms provide ample space for the entire family and feature a luxurious living area with an integrated seating area.

Location:

201 South Studio Drive, Lake Buena Vista, FL 32830-1699

Phone:

(407) 939-5203

Maximum Persons Per Room:

2-8

Room Rates:

- 2 Guests per Cabin: $1209 per person per night or $4809 for the entire trip

- 3 Guests per Cabin (Two adults and one child): $889 per person per night or $5299 for the entire trip.

- 4 Guests per Cabin (Three adults and one child): $749 per night per guest or $5,999 total.

Tip:

Guests can further immerse themselves in a galaxy far, far away by making use of the extensive merchandise collection available onboard the Halcyon starship. Guests can also take a piece of the Star Wars: Galactic Starcruiser experience home with them, thanks to an extensive selection of apparel, collectibles, home goods, and more.

Image: LtPowers

One of the coziest Disney resorts is this luxurious Walt Disney World resort. Nestled in a wooded area, its Northwest motif is immediately apparent upon arrival. The magnificent atrium features a stone fireplace that is 82 feet tall. A cascading waterfall empties into the swimming pool, and you can relax in oversized hot tubs. Your cozy retreat is secluded on the shores of Bay Lake and features restaurants, lounges, a health club, and watercraft rentals.

Disney's Wilderness Lodge offers various accommodations to suit various preferences and needs, but most guests are drawn to the rooms' rustic charm. Each room is decorated with wood-carved furniture, earth tones, and accents of forest creatures.

Location:

901 Timberline Drive, Lake Buena Vista, FL 32830-1000

Phone:

(407) 824-3200

Maximum Persons Per Room:

2-6

Room Rates:

- Standard View - Ranges from $458 to $916 per night, depending on the season
- Standard View – King Bed - Ranges from $465 to $922 per night, depending on the season.

- Nature View - Ranges from $518 to $932 per night, depending on the season

- Nature View – King Bed - Ranges from $523 to $937 per night, depending on the season

- Courtyard View - Ranges from $570 to $946 per night, depending on the season

- Courtyard View – King Bed - Ranges from $570 to $954 per night, depending on the season

- Nature Fireworks View - Ranges from $728 to $1,146 per night, depending on the season

- Nature Fireworks View – King Bed - Ranges from $734 to $1,152 per night, depending on the season

- Standard Room – Club Level - Ranges from $754 to $1,279 per night, depending on the season

- Standard Room – King Bed – Club Level - Ranges from $759 to $1,285 per night, depending on the season

- Deluxe Room – Club Level Access - Ranges from $958 to $1,740 per night, depending on the season

Tip:

Each afternoon, a variety of poolside activities are scheduled. Families can participate in a variety of games and challenges, ranging from chalk art to bingo, while enjoying the water area.

Disney's Yacht Club Resort

This picturesque Disney World Deluxe resort is situated on Crescent Lake. It evokes images of New England seaside splendor, complete with a clapboard-sided lighthouse, and is ideal for guests who wish to unwind in style. It is most well-known for its three-acre Stormalong Bay pool complex, which features a 150-foot slide and sandy bottom. This Disney resort is within walking distance of Epcot and features a variety of recreation options and dining options.

The guest rooms at Disney's Yacht Club are decorated with white furniture and rich jewel tones to complement the resort's nautical theme. The headboards of the bed feature ship's wheel motifs, and the upholstery are embroidered with miniature anchors.

All concierge rooms and suites are located on the fifth floor, which is only accessible to club-level guests. The standard club-level room is comparable to a standard guest room in terms of size and furnishings. Club-level service includes the use of the concierge lounge (Regatta Club) and concierge staff for private check-in and check-out, making dining Priority Seating reservations, planning outings, answering questions, purchasing tickets, arranging transportation, and fulfilling requests for special dining or lodging needs.

Location:

1700 Epcot Resorts Blvd Lake Buena Vista, FL

Phone:

(407) 934-7000

Maximum Persons Per Room:

4-6

Room Rates:

- Standard View - Ranges from $543 to $986 per night, depending on the season

- King Bed - Ranges from $549 to $991 per night, depending on the season

- Garden or Woods View - Ranges from $586 to $1,034 per night, depending on the season

- Water View - Ranges from $684 to $1,118 per night, depending on the season

- Standard View – Club Level - Ranges from $796 to $1,378 per night, depending on the season

- Garden View – Club Level - Ranges from $828 to $1,398 per night, depending on the season

- Water View – Club Level - Ranges from $939 to $1,566 per night, depending on the season

- 2 Bedroom Suite – Club Level Access - Ranges from $2,182 to $3,877 per night, depending on the season

Tip:

The lounge is open daily from 7 a.m. to 10 p.m. and serves a continental breakfast in the morning, light snacks in the afternoon, hot and cold hors d'oeuvres in the evenings, as well as desserts and cordials at night.

Animal Kingdom Lodge Villas - Jambo House and Kidani Village

Image: Tripadvisor/Photo By: Karl83

The Villas at Animal Kingdom Lodge is one of the most popular Homes Away From Home resorts because most rooms offer savannah views. What better way to awaken than to see giraffes, zebras, and gazelles grazing in the open savannah beyond the picture windows.

Although not all buildings offer savannah views, all buildings offer the same picturesque views of the iconic Tree of Life. The buildings are separated into two sections - Jambo House and Kidani Village, named after Kenyan towns. Buildings within Jambo House are located on one side of the resort near Sanaa, while the buildings in Kidani Village are located on the opposite side of the resort near Jiko.

Location:

2901/3701 Osceola Parkway, Lake Buena Vista, FL 32830-1000

Phone:

(407) 938-3000

Maximum Persons Per Room:

4-12

Room Rates:

- Deluxe Studio – Standard View - Ranges from $468 to $838 per night, depending on the season.

- Deluxe Studio – Savanna View - Ranges from $670 to $1,109 per night, depending on the season.

- 1 Bedroom Villa – Standard View - Ranges from $771 to $1,357 per night, depending on the season.

- 1 Bedroom Villa – Savanna View - Ranges from $906 to $1,526 per night, depending on the season.

- 2 Bedroom Villa – Standard View - Ranges from $1,158 to $2,380 per night, depending on the season.

- 2 Bedroom Villa – Savanna View - Ranges from $ 1,366 to $2,841 per night, depending on the season.

- 3 Bedroom Grand Villa – Savanna View - Ranges from $2,629 to $4,542 per night, depending on the season.

Tip:

The standard view rooms face the pool, the garden, or the parking lot. The standard view rooms are available upon request but cannot be guaranteed.

Bay Lake Towers

The Bay Lake Tower of Disney Vacation Club at Disney's Contemporary Resort offers views of the Magic Kingdom and Bay Lake.

This resort features a viewing platform for fireworks and a sky bridge (an elevated walkway on the fourth floor) that connects it to the renowned Contemporary Resort. Bay Lake Tower offers studio units in addition to accommodations with one, two, and three bedrooms. Units with one, two, or three bedrooms have fully equipped kitchens with granite countertops.

Location:

4600 North World Drive, Lake Buena Vista, FL 32830-8413

Phone:

(407) 824-1818

Maximum Persons Per Room:

4-6

Room Rates:

- Deluxe Studio – Standard View - Ranges from $652 to $1,110 per night, depending on the season.

- Deluxe Studio – Lake View - Ranges from $774 to $1,216 per night, depending on the season.

- Deluxe Studio – Theme Park View - Ranges from $870 to $1,348 per night, depending on the season.

- 1-Bedroom Villa – Standard View - Ranges from $956 to $1,565 per night, depending on the season.

- 1-Bedroom Villa – Lake View - Ranges from $972 to $1,645 per night, depending on the season.

- 1-Bedroom Villa – Theme Park View - Ranges from $1,127 to $1,840 per night, depending on the season.

- 2-Bedroom Villa – Standard View - Ranges from $1,253 to $2,719 per night, depending on the season.

- 2-Bedroom Villa – Lake View - Ranges from $1,411 to $2,834 per night, depending on the season.

- 2-Bedroom Villa – Theme Park View3 - Ranges from $1,559 to $3,139 per night, depending on the season.

- -Bedroom Grand Villa – Lake View - Ranges from $2,869 to $4,894 per night, depending on the season.

- 3-Bedroom Grand Villa – Theme Park View - Ranges from $3,094 to $5,382 per night, depending on the season.

Tip:

There are no restaurants in the Bay Lake Tower building, with the exception of the Top of the World Lounge; they are all located in the main building of Disney's Contemporary Resort, which is a short distance away via a bridge.

Image: Tripadvisor/Photo by: mom24kidz

It is the smallest Disney Vacation Club property adjacent to Disney's Wilderness Lodge. The units are warm, inviting, and cozy, and they all share a fantastic theme.

The villa section of the resort has its own separate common area that exudes rustic charm and invites you to relax and read a book. The three-story-tall central rotunda features comfortable seating and a cozy fireplace, extending the theme of the resort's main lobby. A large decorative birdcage and animals carved into log-like "bearing beams" complete the look.

Location:

901 Timberline Drive, Lake Buena Vista, FL 32830

Phone:

(407) 824-3200

Maximum Persons Per Room:

4-8

Room Rates:

- Deluxe Studio - Ranges from $$458 to $916 per night, depending on the season.

- 1 Bedroom Villa - Ranges from $791 to $1,225 per night, depending on the season.

- 2 Bedroom Villa - Ranges from $1,312 to $2,426 per night, depending on the season.

Tip:

The Carolwood Pacific Room, located next to the rotunda, is a particularly inviting area of the villas. This room contains a bit of Disney history, as it displays a few collector's items associated with Walt Disney's passion for steam trains. On select days, a knowledgeable cast member gives brief presentations in the Carolwood Pacific Room, sharing some of the stories associated with the objects. In addition, this area contains additional seating, a few tables, and a couple of checkers game sets for quiet enjoyment.

Disney's Beach Club Villas

This seaside-themed Disney Vacation Club resort is situated on the shores of Crescent Lake. In addition to its own tranquil pool and whirlpool spa, it provides access to the Stormalong Bay Pool complex, regarded as the best Disney offers.

The villas' coastal color palette and casual design reflect the beach theme. Neutral hues of light blue and beige dominate the interior design. Symbols of the beach, such as sand dollars and shells, are dispersed throughout the space, along with Mother of Pearl accents on select pieces of furniture. Each room features sliding doors that lead to a patio or balcony.

Location:

1800 Epcot Resorts Blvd., Lake Buena Vista, FL 32830

Phone:

(407) 934-8000

Maximum Persons Per Room:

4-8

Room Rates:

- Deluxe Studio - Ranges from $543 to $982 per night, depending on the season.

- 1-Bedroom Villa - Ranges from $824 to $1,398 per night, depending on the season.

- 2-Bedroom Villa - Ranges from $1,236 to $2,401 per night, depending on the season.

Tip:

Take your time exploring the resort's three seating areas. The seaside artifacts, including the various weathervanes in the Breezeway, are entertaining to examine.

Image: Tripadvisor/Photo by: Alicathelton

This Disney Vacation Club resort evokes a time when quaint coastal towns were the dream of every vacationer. This expansive resort, along with its sister Boardwalk Resort, features four pools, one of which is an amusement park-themed pool with a water slide resembling a classic wooden roller coaster. The Boardwalk area is filled with restaurants, carnival games, and entertainment options.

The majority of these two-story cottages have a private yard with lovely rose gardens enclosed by a [white picket] fence. It features a king-size bed, a television, a nightstand, and a full bathroom with a hot tub, with a view of the ground floor. A mini-television is available for viewing in the hot tub. Some suites have private balconies instead of a yard with a fence.

Location:

2101 N Epcot Resorts Blvd, Lake Buena Vista, FL 32830

Phone:

(407) 939-6200

Maximum Persons Per Room:

2-8

Room Rates:

- Deluxe Studio – Standard View - Ranges from $596 to $1,044 per night, depending on the season.

- Deluxe Studio – Garden or Pool View - Ranges from $624 to $1,065 per night, depending on the season.

- Deluxe Studio – Boardwalk View - Ranges from $745 to $1,136 per night, depending on the season.

- 1 Bedroom Villa – Garden or Pool View - Ranges from $822 to $1,402 per night, depending on the season.

- 1 Bedroom Villa – Standard View - Ranges from $824 to $1,402 per night, depending on the season.

- 1 Bedroom Villa – Boardwalk View - Ranges from $830 to $1,415 per night, depending on the season.

Tip:

The Boardwalk area is filled with restaurants, carnival games, and entertainment options. The Seaside Cabanas Dining Pavilion features a large collection of old-fashioned cars that are available for viewing during the evening hours. Another popular spot in the Boardwalk area is the location of Madame Tussauds Orlando, located in a former police station. Although it's not an official Disney store, you can still find souvenirs, collectibles, and refreshments.

Copper Creek Villas & Cabins at Disney's Wilderness Lodge

The resort's design incorporates natural elements such as wood and stone and subtle references to the transcontinental railroad inspired by the Pacific Northwest's natural beauty. Each Villa is thoughtfully designed with modern families in mind, featuring full kitchens, increased storage space for personal belongings, and private patios or balconies with scenic views.

Location:

901 Timberline Drive, Lake Buena Vista, FL 32830-1000

Phone:

(407) 824-3200

Maximum Persons Per Room:

4- 12

Room Rates:

- Deluxe Studio - Ranges from $543 to $914 per night, depending on the season.

- Deluxe One-Bedroom Villa - Ranges from $836 to $1,376 per night, depending on the season.

- Deluxe Two-Bedroom Villa - Ranges from $1,331 to $2,395 per night, depending on the season.

- Cabins - Ranges from $2,518 to $4,854 per night, depending on the season.

- 3 Bedroom Grand Villa - Ranges from $2,658 to $5,128 per night, depending on the season.

Tip:

Some Deluxe Studios offer the option to reserve a walk-in shower.

Disney's Old Key West Resort

This Disney Vacation Club resort has the colors, palm trees, and atmosphere of the Florida Keys. This expansive resort features four pools: a main pool with a sandcastle motif, water recreation, a restaurant, and meticulously manicured grounds.

The rooms' plush armchairs and bedding invite guests to kick back and relax. The Old Key West Resort offers spacious living areas with breathtaking views of the Lake Buena Vista golf course, surrounding woodlands, or waterways. Full bathrooms have ceramic tile floors and storage space beneath the sink in the vanity unit. Private balconies and patios provide access to the picturesque view. There are handicap-accessible rooms available.

Location:

1510 North Cove Road, Lake Buena Vista, FL 32830

Phone:

(407) 827-7700

Maximum Persons Per Room:

4-12

Room Rates:

- Deluxe Studio - Ranges from $458 to $774 per night, depending on the season.

- 1 Bedroom Villa – Ranges from $623 to $1,099 per night, depending on the season.

- 2 Bedroom Villa – Ranges from $892 to $1,719 per night, depending on the season.

- 3 Bedroom Grand Villa – Ranges from $1,908 to $3,081 per night, depending on the season.

Tip:

Each afternoon, a variety of poolside activities are scheduled. Families can participate in a variety of games and challenges, ranging from arts and crafts to trivia, while they enjoy the water area.

Disney's Polynesian Villas & Bungalows

This tropical resort is a tropical island paradise in the heart of the magic. It is the first Disney resort to sit atop the waters of the Seven Seas Lagoon and features iconic mid-20th-century architecture. This resort's Deluxe Studios are the largest among all Walt Disney World Resorts. The proximity to the monorail makes transportation simple.

One bathroom in their Deluxe Studios has a shower and sink, while the other has a sink and tub/shower. In addition to kitchenettes, each unit features a pull-down armoire bed with Lilo and Stitch artwork.

There are 20 bungalows, each measuring 1650 square feet and featuring two full bathrooms, a kitchen, in-unit laundry facilities, a living room, and a dining area.

Location:

1600 Seven Seas Drive, Lake Buena Vista, FL 32830

Phone:

(407) 824-2000

Maximum Persons Per Room:

5-8

Room Rates:

- Deluxe Studio – Standard View – Ranges from $662 to $1,184 per night, depending on the season.

- Deluxe Studio – Lake View – Ranges from $835 to $1,438 per night, depending on the season.

- Bungalow – Ranges from $3,309 to $6,146 per night, depending on the season.

Tip:

When not reserved by Disney Vacation Club Members, all DVC accommodations are available for rent.

Disney's Riviera Resort

This new resort is the 15th Disney Vacation Club property and features approximately 300 units of a variety of accommodations. The Disney Skyliner transports guests between the resort and other Walt Disney World locations.

This Deluxe Disney Vacation Club Resort offers approximately 300 vacation homes that are suitable for families. The resort's artwork references a variety of well-known Disney characters.

Location:

1080 Esplanade Avenue, Lake Buena Vista, FL 32830

Phone:

(407) 828-7030

Maximum Persons Per Room:

5-12

Room Ranges:

- Tower Studio Ranges from $453 to $814 per night, depending on the season.

- Deluxe Studio – Standard View Ranges from $688 to $1,133 per night, depending on the season.

- Deluxe Studio – Preferred View Ranges from $749 to $1,250 per night, depending on the season.

- 1 Bedroom Villa – Standard View Ranges from $944 to $1,526 per night, depending on the season.

- 1 Bedroom Villa – Preferred View – Standard View Ranges from $1,032 to $1,798 per night, depending on the season.

- 2 Bedroom Villa – Standard View – Standard View Ranges from $1,548 to $2,446 per night, depending on the season.

- 2 Bedroom Villa – Preferred View – Standard View Ranges from $1,692 to $2,807 per night, depending on the season.

- 3 Bedroom Grand Villa– Standard View Ranges from $3,102 to $5,165 per night, depending on the season.

Tip:

Guests staying at Disney's Riviera Resort now have access to Disney Skyliner, a state-of-the-art gondola system, to travel to Epcot or Disney's Hollywood Studios. The system connects Disney's Hollywood Studios and Epcot with Disney's Art of Animation Resort, Disney's Pop Century Resort, and Disney's Caribbean Beach Resort.

Disney's Saratoga Springs Resort & Spa

This Victorian-themed Disney Vacation Club resort is modeled after the horse-racing-rich region of upstate New York. You'll notice the influence of the horse community in the statues, room decorations, and unexpected touches like the hourly clock chime. Due to its proximity to Disney Springs, you will have access to a variety of restaurants and shops.

Studio and one-bedroom units at Disney's Saratoga Springs Resort and Spa can accommodate up to four guests, while two-bedroom units and Grand Villas can accommodate up to twelve. Each unit can accommodate one infant younger than 3 years old in a crib.

Location:

1960 Broadway, Lake Buena Vista, FL 32830

Phone:

(407) 827-1100

Room Rates:

- Deluxe Studio - Ranges from $459 to $770 per night, depending on the season.
- Deluxe Studio – Preferred - Ranges from $531 to $881 per night, depending on the season.
- 1 Bedroom Villa - Ranges from $622 to $1,088 per night, depending on the season.
- 1 Bedroom Villa – Preferred - Ranges from $712 to $1,227 per night, depending on the season.
- 2 Bedroom Villa - Ranges from $891 to $1,713 per night, depending on the season.
- 2 Bedroom Villa – Preferred - Ranges from $1,076 to $2,006 per night, depending on the season.

- Treehouse Villa - Ranges from $1,114 to $2,134 per night, depending on the season.

- 3-Bedroom Grand Villa - Ranges from $1,908 to $3,074 per night, depending on the season.

- 3-Bedroom Grand Villa – Preferred - Ranges from $2,206 to $3,477 per night, depending on the season.

Tip:

Free motorcoach transportation to theme parks and water parks and water launch service to Disney Springs venues. This resort is expansive, and guests should be aware that an internal bus is available for travel between the various areas.

Villas at Disney's Grand Floridian Resort & Spa

Photo by: Tripadvisor/Justinyyhong

Because of their luxurious amenities, Victorian-style furnishings, and fine finishes, the Villas at Disney's Grand Floridian Resort & Spa is the crown jewel of Disney Vacation Club.

The rooms feature a predominance of elegance and sophistication. The extremely clean and comfortable accommodations feature pastel hues that complement the neutral hues. More whimsical touches (such as beautiful murals of Dumbo hidden in a stowaway bed) add a touch of whimsy to the villas' otherwise Victorian ambiance. All rooms are spacious and feature granite countertops, crown molding, and televisions mounted in the bathroom mirrors.

Location:

4401 Floridian Way, Lake Buena Vista, FL 32830

Phone:

(407) 824-3000

Maximum Persons Per Room:

5-12

Room Rates:

- Resort Studio – Standard View - Ranges from $794 to $1,279 per night, depending on the season.

- Deluxe Studio – Standard View - Ranges from $794 to$1,279 per night, depending on the season.

- Resort Studio – Lagoon View - Ranges from $808 to $1,362 per night, depending on the season.

- Deluxe Studio – Lake View - Ranges from $808 to $1,362 per night, depending on the season.

- Resort Studio – Theme Park View - Ranges from $930 to $1,630 per night, depending on the season.

- 1 Bedroom Villa – Standard View - Ranges from $1,070 to $1,809 per night, depending on the season.

- 1 Bedroom Villa – Lake View - Ranges from $1,221 to $2,027 per night, depending on the season.

- 2 Bedroom Villa – Standard View - Ranges from $1,738 to $2,816 per night, depending on the season.

- 2 Bedroom Villa – Lake View - Ranges from $1,902 to $3,274 per night, depending on the season.

- 3 Bedroom Grand Villa – Lake View - Ranges from $3,351 to $5,929 per night, depending on the season.

Tip:

In 2008, Jingles was rededicated in a ceremony honoring Julie Andrews for her contributions to Disneyland and Disney films. While waiting for an elevator at the Villas, keep your eyes peeled for Andrews' Mary Poppins umbrella.

When the room rates were compiled, they were accurate. It is common for Disney to change rates and policies without notice, although it is uncommon. Prices are per room, per night, and there are no additional fees for guests up to the maximum occupancy. A single infant under 3 years old sleeping in a crib does not count toward the maximum occupancy.

Alternative Accommodations

On occasion, you may be required to stay in a hotel off-site while visiting Walt Disney World. These instances can range from the need for more space than a hotel room provides to the need to adhere to a strict budget. With fluctuating travel demand, it could be difficult to find available rooms at Disney World Resort Hotels.

You can certainly stay "on property" at Disney and receive perks such as free park transportation. You can also have a magical experience by staying at one of these off-property hotels. Some off-property hotels offer the same advantages as Disney resort hotels, including proximity to the theme parks, shuttle service to the parks, and magical amenities such as character breakfasts, on-site water parks, and great pools.

The following are some of the off-property hotels that are close to the Walt Disney World Resort:

Wyndham (Garden) Lake Buena Vista

This hotel offers a slightly cheaper rate and fewer room amenities, but if you intend to spend your time in the parks, you will have everything you need at a very low price. The hotel is within walking distance of Disney Springs, where you can catch a bus to the parks and where you can find excellent dining and shopping just outside the door. The Wyndham also features a number of themed rooms with Disney-specific touches, such as Finding Nemo and Cars-inspired decor.

The main pool is a great place to unwind after a long day in the park, but there are also smaller pools for children. There is a fitness center on-site for those who like to stay active while on vacation, as well as an arcade for those who don't. This hotel does not have a lounge, but the continental breakfast with fresh oranges and coffee is still pleasant.

Location:

1850(B) Hotel Plaza Boulevard, Lake Buena Vista, FL, 32830

Phone:

(407) 828-4444

Maximum Persons Per Room:

3-4

Room Rates:

- Disney View, 2 Queen Beds - Ranges from $90 to $179 per night, depending on the season.

- Lake Buena Vista View, 1 King Bed - Ranges from $115 to $159 per night, depending on the season.

- Lake Buena Vista View, 2 Queen Beds - Ranges from $124 to $179 per night, depending on the season.

Tip:

When traveling during the summer, save your room for a weeknight and stay away from theme park crowds on Sundays. If you find yourself in a Disney hotel on a weeknight, just head to the park around noon, when most people go home to rest before returning to their hotels after dark.

Hilton Orlando Buena Vista Palace

Also a short walk away from Disney Springs is the Hilton Orlando Buena Vista Palace. This beautiful hotel has a lot to offer your family, including a great pool with a lazy river, spacious suites to accommodate larger families, and a panoramic view of the Disney Springs resort area from some of the rooms.

Location:

1900 E Buena Vista Dr, Lake Buena Vista, FL 32830

Phone:

(407) 827-2727

Maximum Persons Per Room:

5-7

Room Rates:

- 1 King Bed - Resort View - Ranges from $217 to $348 per night, depending on the season.

- 1 King Bed - Disney Springs View - Ranges from $317 to $399 per night, depending on the season.

- 1 King Bed - Epcot Fireworks View - Ranges from $307 to $359 per night, depending on the season.

- 2 Queen Beds - Resort View - Ranges from $225 to $312 per night, depending on the season.

- 2 Queen Beds - Disney Springs View - Ranges from $326 to $378 per night, depending on the season.

- 2 Queen Beds - Epcot Fireworks View - Ranges from $312 to $380 per night, depending on the season.

Tip:

Disney transportation shuttle available daily to and from the hotel and Disney theme parks

Waldorf Astoria Orlando

The dreamy Waldorf Astoria Orlando is the place to stay for a luxurious Disney vacation. This resort has food choices and activities for every member of the family. Plus, with complimentary transportation to and from the Disney parks. You can also purchase your Disney park tickets on-site at the concierge desk.

Location:

1005 West Buena Vista Drive, Lake Buena Vista, FL 32830

Phone:

(407) 939-1300

Maximum Persons Per Room:

3-4

Room Rates:

- Deluxe Room - Ranges from $261 to $355 per night, depending on the season.

- 1 King Bed Deluxe Room - Disney View - Ranges from $386 to $485 per night, depending on the season.

- 2 Queen Beds Deluxe Room - Ranges from $474 to $570 per night, depending on the season.

- 2 Queen Beds Oversized Deluxe Room - Ranges from $461 to $552 per night, depending on the season.

- 2 Queen Beds Deluxe Room - Golf View - Ranges from $473 to $567 per night, depending on the season.

- 2 Queen Beds Deluxe Room - Disney View - Ranges from $589 to $795 per night, depending on the season.

Tip:

Get the extra magic hours option on your tickets by staying at the Waldorf Astoria Orlando. You can enjoy an extra hour in the park an unlimited number of times each day, whereas the regular guests get just three hours a day.

Four Seasons Resort

The Four Seasons Resort Orlando is located within Disney World's gates. You will have breathtaking views of the lake, access to beautifully landscaped gardens, and a selection of pools. There is a lazy river, family pool, playground, and water slides for children. For your convenience, the hotel offers a complimentary shuttle service to Magic Kingdom, Animal Kingdom, Hollywood Studios, and Epcot.

Location:

10100 Dream Tree Boulevard, Lake Buena Vista, Orlando, FL 32836

Phone:

(407) 313-7777

Maximum Persons Per Room:

3-5

Room Rates:

- Four Seasons Room - Ranges from $219 to $558 per night, depending on the season.

- Golden Oak View Room - Ranges from $219 to $558 per night, depending on the season.

- Lakeview Room - Ranges from $219 to $498 per night, depending on the season.

- Park View Room - Ranges from $219 to $498 per night, depending on the season.

Tip:

Ask for a room facing the Disney hotel pools. You'll get the chance to watch all of Disney Springs as you swim.

Holiday Inn Orlando

Situated in Disney Springs, Holiday Inn Orlando features a wide range of facilities. All rooms boast contemporary designs, elegant bathrooms, and views of the pool. The hotel offers outdoor swimming pools, a whirlpool, a cocktail lounge, and a fitness center. Free shuttle to Disney World parks is available to all guests.

Location:

1805 Hotel Plaza Boulevard, Lake Buena Vista,

Phone:

(407) 828-8888

Maximum Persons Per Room:

3-6

Room Rates:

- 1 King Bed - Ranges from $105 to $120 per night, depending on the season.

- 2 Queen Beds - Ranges from $107 to $120 per night, depending on the season.

- 1 King Bed - Pool View - Ranges from $109 to $115 per night, depending on the season.

- 1 King Bed - Fireworks View - Ranges from $135 to $169 per night, depending on the season.

- 2 Queen Beds - Fireworks View - Ranges from $159 to $229 per night, depending on the season.

- 2 Queen Bed - Disney Spring View - Ranges from $155 to $239 per night, depending on the season.

Tip:

Take advantage of the shuttle service that connects Disney Springs and this hotel. The shuttle runs every 30 minutes between 7 a.m. and 11 p.m. and also stops at Disney theme parks. This route will bring you directly to Disney Springs from all three of the theme parks.

Benefits of Staying On-Site

There are several benefits to staying on Walt Disney World property, including:

1. Lightning Lane Selections

Guests staying on-site will have a significant advantage when it comes to Individual Lightning Lane selections, as they can make their selections at 7 a.m., whereas guests staying off-site will have to wait until the park opens to make their selections.

And, despite the fact that only two or three attractions in each park are eligible for this pay-to-ride service, as you can see from the list below, it includes some of the most popular attractions in each park:

Magic Kingdom:
- Seven Dwarfs Mine Train
- Space Mountain

Epcot
- Frozen Ever After
- Remy's Ratatouille Adventure
- Guardians of the Galaxy: Cosmic Rewind

Hollywood Studios
- Mickey & Minnie's Runaway Railway
- Star Wars: Rise of the Resistance

Animal Kingdom
- Avatar Flight of Passage
- Expedition Everest – Legend of the Forbidden Mountain

Attractions commonly run out of Individual Lightning Lane passes before the park opens, meaning you must use the standby line if you are staying off-site and want to ride. In addition, since you will not be eligible for Early Theme Park Entry if you stay off-site, you should anticipate a lengthy wait. Early Entry indicates that Magic Kingdom or Disney's Hollywood Studios (for example) open daily to resort guests at 8:30 a.m. and 8 a.m., respectively, and 30 minutes later to non-resort guests.

2. Additional Days for Dining Reservation

All Walt Disney Resort guests can make dining reservations sixty days in advance. This benefit can be extremely useful if you're attempting to secure the most coveted reservations. Due to the fact that on-site guests make reservations 60+10 days in advance, some of the most popular reservations and character meals will be unavailable at 60 days.

3. Stay Later at the Parks

Extended Evening Hours allow you to stay later than the general public in the parks and ride all attractions with minimal wait times. Extended Evening Hours are offered one night per week at Disney's Magic Kingdom and EPCOT. Occasionally Hollywood Studios is also included. During this night, the park is typically open for an extra two hours, from 9:00 p.m. to 11:00 p.m. or 10:00 p.m. to midnight.

Guests staying at one of the Deluxe Resorts, Deluxe Villas, Walt Disney World Swan and Dolphin, Swan Reserve, or Disney's Shades of Green may utilize Extended Evening Hours. Unfortunately, guests staying at Value or Moderate resorts are unable to enjoy this amenity.

4. Free Parking and Complimentary Transportation

If you stay on-site at Disney World and drive to the theme parks, parking is complimentary at both the resorts and the parks. Saving $25 per day on park parking is a nice perk. In addition to the savings on parking, staying on-site and having access to Disney transportation to get you to the parks has additional non-monetary benefits, such as making it easier for groups to split up without having to worry about dropping off and picking up members of their party.

Additionally, resort guests who drive to the parks are not charged extra for valet parking. Simply park your vehicle and take the complimentary Disney transportation system directly to the Magic Kingdom or Epcot.

5. Charging Privileges

Disney provides convenient charging privileges for resort guests. This means that you can charge purchases made while shopping or dining at most locations on the property to your room. To simplify things, you use the same MagicBand or Key to the World card (essentially your hotel room key) to enter the parks.

When you check into your resort room, a hold will be placed on the credit card associated with the room for the amount due at check-in, plus $100 for incidental charges. As you charge items to your room, if your balance exceeds the initial $100 hold placed on your credit card, additional $100 holds will be placed incrementally. The hold on your credit card should not exceed the amount you currently owe plus an additional $100, although it may take a while for the hold to "fall off."

This eliminates the need to carry a wallet throughout the day, as dining and entertainment expenses can be charged to your room.

6. Location

Depending on the resort you select, you may be able to walk to a Disney park, which is not possible if you stay off-site. You may want to return to your resort in the middle of the afternoon after spending the morning in the Florida sun. Who could blame you? Particularly if you intend to return in the evening and stay late to watch the fireworks.

A significant advantage of staying at a Disney Resort is the convenience of returning to your resort. For example, if you are staying at Magic Kingdom, the bus stop is directly outside the park's entrance. If you were staying off-site, however, you would be required to return to the Transportation and Ticket Center. Then you would have to locate the location where your off-property shuttle picked you up and wait for it. Otherwise, you would have to navigate the enormous parking lot.

Typically, if you were staying at a Disney Resort, you would be fast asleep in your resort room.

7. Saves Time

If you're unfamiliar with the Lake Buena Vista region, staying on Disney property will save you time.

Occasionally, you may feel as though you've waited forever for a bus. Or you may not know the best way to get from Magic Kingdom to Epcot. But these instances will likely be insignificant in the grand scheme of things. In addition, you will not be stuck in traffic like those waiting to pay at the park's entrance. Disney buses have a dedicated entrance lane to the parks.

Moreover, a separate bus lane begins as you approach Disney Springs if you are traveling by bus. It saves a tremendous amount of time on a busy evening. In addition, you are on Disney property, which has few traffic lights and wide, multi-lane roads. As you leave the property, traffic becomes more congested, and those lengthy Florida traffic lights are everywhere.

8. Free WiFi

On-property WiFi access is available at the Walt Disney World resorts. Simply request the password from the cast member at check-in. Free and unlimited service is ideal for guests who are constantly on the move. It can also be useful if you're looking for information about your vacation plans or the day's free attractions.

With access to multiple parks, resorts, and Downtown Disney locations, Disney has enhanced this feature over time to make it better than ever.

9. Resort Recreation and Upgrades

Another advantage of staying at a Walt Disney World Resort is the abundance of activities. Each resort provides complimentary recreational activities for guests to enjoy during their stay. You can participate in a fitness class, swim in the resort's pool, play tennis or basketball, or bike around the resort's track. Take a cooking class or visit the spa if you wish to be more active during your vacation.

Some resorts even provide a view of a theme park and Disney transportation. Some resorts provide upgraded amenities such as enhanced views, park access, luxury, etc.

10. The Disney Bubble

While it is not a mysterious alien planet, there are benefits to living in the Disney bubble. You get the impression as soon as you set foot on the property that it operates somewhat differently from other places you're used to. The air smells fresher, the food tastes better, and the population is happier. Perhaps it's the hotel's proximity to the theme parks or the way the cast members go out of their way to make each day extra special. Or perhaps Disney has a way of captivating the mind and uplifting the spirit.

When you return home, the illusion bursts, and the real world sets in. And at that point, your craving for the magical sensation that can only be found when you are fully immersed in your Disney vacation begins all over again, which is why millions of guests return year after year seeking more.

When comparing straight savings to savings, Disney Resort hotels are always going to be more expensive, and you can always find a better deal off-site. If that is your primary concern, then you are probably best served to stay at a non-Disney hotel or rental property.

That being said, there is nothing like staying on-site. You can walk to the park or hop on a ferry to the Disney Springs area without worrying about driving, parking, or fighting traffic. Plus, staying on-site is a lot less hassle than getting through the parks daily from off-site travel. It's also more convenient than trying to navigate your way around Downtown Disney for dinner every night.

All told, with all these benefits of staying on-site, the convenience, dining options, beautiful atmosphere, amazing cast members, and everything else staying on-site provides.

The following is one of the best attractions at each of the parks at Walt Disney World:

Magic Kingdom

Seven Dwarfs Mine Train

Image: Josh Hallett from Winter Haven

The Snow White story is presented in a novel, contemporary way on this family-friendly roller coaster. Visitors ride a brand-new ride system on a train as it takes them on a musical tour of the dwarfs' diamond mine. Visitors will feel every bend in the track because the cars rock back and forth just like real mine cars. The cars are designed to give the impression that they were manually carved out of wood by the dwarfs using an ax.

Audio-animatronic characters and movie music round out the narrative and take the audience into the forest with Snow White and her friends. Visitors will witness the dwarves navigating the mountain on their "mine train" and interacting with Snow White and one another.

Date Open:

May 28, 2014

Wait Times:

60-90 minutes

Length of Ride:

2 minutes 30 seconds

Lightning Lane:

Yes

Age Restriction:

This attraction is a roller coaster; therefore, children under 2 must be accompanied by an adult. Minors must be at least 32 inches tall to ride without a parent present.

Health Restriction:

Expectant mothers should not ride as sharp turns; sudden drops and stops are to be expected.

Did You Know:

20,000 Leagues Under the Sea, Pooh's Playful Spot was previously in this location but was moved to Fantasyland in 2011 to make more room for Seven Dwarfs Mine Train.

Pirates of the Caribbean

Image: HarshLight from San Jose

The massive fortress at the far end of Adventureland houses the Pirates of the Caribbean ride. The line winds and turns in a cool, dark, underground cavern that leads to the boat ride. After a close encounter with Davy Jones and Blackbeard, you'll float through a cave before taking a swift, dark plunge.

As your boat enters the main area, you'll find yourself in the middle of a battle with cannon shots flying by. Captain Barbossa himself yells orders from the pirate ship. Be on the lookout for Captain Jack Sparrow. When the ride is over, he will be perched atop a mountain of loot after emerging from a barrel and peeking around a mannequin.

The original Audio-animatronics are somewhat basic in comparison to the most recent additions, but the detail is amazing. The pirate swinging his leg from the bridge has realistic-looking clothing, hairy legs, and a hairy head.

Date Open:

December 15, 1973

Wait Times:

15-30 minutes

Length of Ride:

8 minutes, 30 seconds

Lightning Lane:

Yes

Age Restriction:

This attraction is a dark ride; therefore, children under 7 must be accompanied by an adult. Minors must be at least 40 inches tall to ride without a parent present.

Health Restriction:

Expectant mothers should not ride as a boat is lifted off the water several feet at a time.

Did You Know:

This attraction was closed for refurbishment in October 2018 with new animatronics, but temporarily reopened in December 2018 with the old animatronics when the new ones broke down.

Image: Kaleeb18

After more than 40 years, Space Mountain is still amazingly popular. It's quite easy compared to the rollercoasters of today. Although it has no upside-down loops and moves at a slower speed than its more contemporary competitors (28.7 mph), the theming makes it unique.

As you careen along the crooked and winding track, it's as pitch-black as night, there are "stars" everywhere, and you're in orbit. The attraction has 60 speakers installed with "Starry-O Phonic Sound," which allows visitors to hear "a zippy musical track, the whoosh of passing asteroids, and the rush of interstellar traffic."

Before you know it, your hair is a complete mess, you're struggling to get out of the rocket, and you're making plans to ride Space Mountain repeatedly.

Date Open:

January 15, 1975

Wait Times:

50-60 minutes

Length of Ride:

2 minutes, 30 seconds

Lightning Lane:

Yes

Age Restrictions:

Children under eight years old are required to be accompanied by an adult. Minors must be at least 44 inches tall to ride when accompanied by an adult.

Health Restriction:

Those with neck problems or heart and back ailments should not ride.

Did You Know:

This attraction is located inside the massive communication tower at the end of Tomorrowland. The idea was to use the facade and create something futuristic. When it opened, Space Mountain was the first indoor roller coaster in the world. It is also America's first roller coaster to be in the dark!

Haunted Mansion

Image: Flickr user/daryl_mitchell Regina

Open since 1970, the Haunted Mansion is a haunt that can't be beaten. It's breathtakingly beautiful, and the lines are often ungodly long.

The queue takes you through some of the manor's most prominent rooms, where you'll encounter your fair share of ghosts, including a plump ghost sitting in his rocking chair and a portrait that makes you think twice about ever leaving. You'll also see the spooky couple from The Legend of Sleepy Hollow, the "Indian" lady from Pinocchio, and a host of other chilling characters.

As you walk deeper into the mansion, each room presents haunted visions of painted actors in costumes who will come alive when disturbed by your movement or noise.

Date Open:

October 1, 1971

Wait Times:

15-30 minutes

Length of Ride:

7 minutes, 30 seconds

Lightning Lane:

Yes

Age Restrictions:

Children under eight years old are required to be accompanied by an adult. Minors must be at least 29 inches tall to ride with a parent present.

Health Restriction:

Expectant mothers should not ride as there are many quick movements. Also, those with heart and back ailments should not ride.

Did You Know:

A more recent addition to the Haunted Mansion was The Hatbox Ghost, which was only seen for about five years before it disappeared into obscurity again. The group responsible for its removal (a group of Imagineers) was fired but was later reinstated after a lawsuit from their original employer.

Disney's Hollywood Studios
The Twilight Zone Tower of Terror

Image: Wikimedia Commons/Micha L. Rieser

After passing through an elevator shaft, riders of the free-fall thrill ride The Twilight Zone Tower of Terror experience a series of random drops from various heights. After being abandoned on that fateful Halloween night, the hotel's lobby appears frozen in time, and the attraction captures the glitz and glamour of the golden age of Hollywood. While the Tower of Terror offers classic thrills and an incredible view of Hollywood Studios just before the drop (especially at night), which really sets it apart from the competition, it is a little spooky, and those drops aren't for everyone.

This attraction is worthwhile to try if you don't mind the drops. Despite the fact that most of the drops are more gradual, it appears as if you are falling quickly. The best part is the moment you take a photo with your "friends" and family at the end.

Date Open:

July 22, 1994

Wait Times:

30-60 minutes

Length of Ride:

5 Minutes

Lightning Lane:

Yes

Age Restrictions:

Children under eight years old are required to be accompanied by an adult. Minors must be at least 44 inches tall to ride with a parent present.

Health Restriction:

Expectant mothers should not ride as there are many quick movements. Also, those with heart and back ailments should not ride.

Did You Know:

This attraction is scary enough that it used to be the only attraction (that was not a simulator) where you could get a ticket holder's name tattooed on your body.

Star Tours is a motion simulator ride. This attraction takes you on a journey to the final frontier, where you'll meet several memorable characters, including the droids R2-D2, C-3PO, BB-8, and pilot Captain Rex. The plot of the attraction is that a rogue band of Imperial Stormtroopers kidnapped Princess Leia and R2-D2 to use them as hostages. Despite having lost control of R2-D2, they are determined to obtain the blueprints for the Death Star, the Empire's ultimate weapon. It is up to Captain Rex to save them in time before an impending attack by Darth Vader and his minions.

The attraction is in a 3-D environment and takes you all over the "Star Wars" universe – from Tatooine to Coruscant and even to a trash compactor, where you'll find yourself face-to-face with Chewbacca. If you're looking for an adventure, Star Tours will not disappoint. The newly updated ride features many new starships for your travel pleasure.

Date Open:

December 1989

Wait Times:

40-60 minutes (Original Ride) 10-15 minutes (New Ride)

Length of Ride:

5 minutes, 10 seconds

Lightning Lane:

Yes (Original) Yes (New)

Age Restrictions:

Children under eight years old are required to be accompanied by an adult. Minors must be at least 40 inches tall to ride with a parent present.

Health Restriction:

Expectant mothers should not ride as there are many quick movements. Also, those with heart and back ailments should not ride.

Did You Know:

There was a lot of debate between the Imagineers and Disney executives over whether or not the attraction should be an actual ride in the theme park or a simulator. After much deliberation, it was decided that Star Tours would become an actual ride in which you would be able to view some famous sets and creatures of "Star Wars." While this decision had little impact on the attraction itself, it did cause much controversy among fans who were hoping for a simulator to finally provide them with their favorite "Star Wars" characters.

Rock 'n' Roller Coaster Starring Aerosmith

Rock 'n' Roller Coaster Starring Aerosmith is among Disney's most thrilling attractions. Aerosmith's legendary rock music is paired with this extreme roller coaster to create a high-speed thrill ride that will literally rock 'n' roll riders.

This indoor roller coaster features a high-speed launch of 0-60 mph in 2.8 seconds, three inversions, rock-concert lighting, and an Aerosmith soundtrack blaring from 120 onboard speakers in each coaster train — all firsts for a Walt Disney World attraction.

Date Open:

July 30, 1999

Wait Times:

15-40 minutes

Length of Ride:

1 minute, 22 seconds

Lightning Lane:

Yes

Age Restrictions:

Children under the age of seven must be accompanied by an adult at least 14 years old. Minors must be at least 48 inches tall to ride with a parent present.

Health Restriction:

This is a high-speed attraction, so expectant mothers should not ride as there are many quick movements. Additionally, those with heart and back ailments should not ride.

Did You Know:

When this attraction first opened, a real person appeared in the pre-show video for Aerosmith. He would retrieve a guitar for the group and deliver it to their "limo." For each never-ending group of riders, day after day, it was the same thing. They would know it was the same guy and call him "The Guitar Guy." Little did they know, he wasn't a guy at all. He was, in fact, Michael L. Williams, who worked for Walt Disney World as a sound engineer and showed producer at the time.

Toy Story Land

Guests can enter the worlds of their favorite films, beginning with Toy Story Land, at Disney's Hollywood Studios. This new 11-acre property transports guests to Andy's backyard, where they can enjoy the outdoors. Guests will feel as if they have been shrunk to the size of a toy, surrounded by oversized toys assembled by Andy using his vivid imagination. Andy has created the ideal setting for this land using toys such as building blocks, plastic buckets, shovels, and game board pieces. Andy liked to play with toys, so he took the ideas of the toys and made them real.

These big-toy versions of Andy's toys embody his imaginative playtime. Andy likes to imagine things, and that is evident in Toy Story Land, which features a variety of interactive toys that invite guests to imagine and create their own adventures. For daring adventures among the giant toys, guests can climb through a huge garage door entrance into many new rides, including Slinky Dog Dash – a roller coaster attraction starring Slinky Dog and his favorite toy friends (Slinky Dog and friends are not included) – and Alien Swirling Saucers, which features flying saucers that spin with the help of little green aliens. Guests can also enjoy an out-of-this-world experience with Toy Story Mania!, a 4D attraction that puts guests in the middle of the Toy Story Midway Games Play Set and offers an opportunity to play carnival games using a variety of "toys," including ping pong balls, eggs, water guns, and beach balls.

The Sarge will entertain guests and the Green Army Man Drum Corps, who will march through the land multiple times per day and stop to play "Sarge Says" and other games with a larger-than-life Pixar ball and crayons. Guests will also have the option to participate in Andy's Backyard's interactive "boot camp" to determine if they have what it takes to become an official recruit.

Date Open:

June 30, 2018

Mickey & Minnie's Runaway Railway

Image: Jeremy Thompson

Mickey & Minnie's Runaway Railway is a new attraction coming to Disney's Hollywood Studios. The attraction, which is being built on what was once the site of the park's Studio Backlot Tour, will feature a new world of characters and experiences inspired by Mickey Mouse animated shorts.

Mickey and Minnie are in the middle of preparing for a picnic when they suddenly find themselves on an unexpected adventure—launched from inside their own home! The dynamic duo embarks upon a musical tour that includes special appearances by some familiar friends—Donald Duck, Goofy, Pluto, and Chip 'n' Dale—along with some surprising new characters.

The attraction includes an innovative, new technology that makes it feel like cartoon shorts are jumping off the screen. And with an original story and unique experiences, it is a whole new way to see Mickey and Minnie like never before.

Date Open:

March 4, 2020

Lightning Lane:

Yes

Age Restrictions:

No height requirement exists, but those younger than 7 years old must be accompanied by an adult.

Health Restriction:

Those with heart or back issues should not ride.

Did You Know:

The Mickey and Minnie's Runaway Railway attraction will feature a new original story and a new innovation – the first Disney attraction to use augmented reality. Similar to how Tony Stark created an early version of JARVIS using his computerized eyeglasses in the movie "Iron Man," Mickey Mouse has invented his own set of goggles that use augmented reality to help him and Minnie Mouse with their latest adventure.

Image:Eden, Janine and Jim from New York City

Disney's moving simulator ride, Dinosaur, is housed in the museum-like Dino Institute, where "the future is truly in the past" and where "the past is truly the future." Informative fossil displays precede entrance to the Institute. The waiting area's walls are covered with life-size replicas of actual dinosaur skeletons. This room's focal point is an enormous Carnotaurus skeleton.

Bill Nye, the Science Guy, sets the stage for your adventure by narrating the theory that fiery meteor showers annihilated the dinosaurs 65 million years ago. The pre-show film is a commercial for the Dino Institute. Here, visitors learn about the rebellious Dr. Grant Seeker's plan. Before you are sent back in time, he requests that you return the last Iguanodon before the meteors destroy the Earth.

Guests proceed to the loading area to board the 12-seat Time Rovers and embark on an exciting journey through time. This moving simulator ride bounces, bumps, and careens through a prehistoric forest, where you'll encounter a number of astounding Audio-animatronic dinosaur specimens and fantastic special effects designed to stimulate all of your senses.

Date Open:

April 22, 1998

Wait Times:

30-60 minutes

Length of Ride:

3 minutes, 30 seconds (15 minutes including pre-show)

Lightning Lane:

Yes

Age Restrictions:

Children under the age of seven must be accompanied by an adult at least 14 years old. Minors must be at least 40 inches tall to ride.

Health Restriction:

This is a moving simulator ride, so expectant mothers should not ride. Additionally, those with heart and back ailments should not ride.

Did You Know:

"Dinosaur" was one of the first Disney attractions that utilized computer-aided special effects and Audio-Animatronics technology in order to create a realistic prehistoric environment using animatronic dinosaurs and a variety of other special effects.

Avatar Flight of Passage

Image:Eden, Janine and Jim from New York City

"Avatar Flight of Passage" is a breathtaking attraction where you will soar through the air on an epic aerial assault, fighting fierce battles with the Na'vi and their Banshees.

"Avatar Flight of Passage" consists of two distinct experiences. The first is the Na'vi River Journey, which takes place under the stars and across a remote ravine. Guests will be able to experience this journey in a 16-passenger boat that is suspended above the ravine and propelled by rocket power. The boat will take you on a thrilling adventure through lush forests and wild rapids – all while dodging tree limbs and rocks in your path. You may even encounter blue banshees (an "avatar" of a creature that dwells in the forest) as well as a host of other exotic Na'vi creatures during your adventure.

The second flight takes riders on an aerial assault of the hostile jungle using a combination of body-contoured seats, strap-in harnesses, and powerful rocket thrusters. This is followed by an exhilarating free fall back to the ground, where guests will be greeted by their Na'vi hosts. The experience ends with warriors singing the "Na'Vi Anthem" to celebrate your courage and bravery during your journey.

Guests who choose not to ride "Avatar Flight of Passage" can also enjoy "Na'Vi River Journey," which is a family-friendly boat ride that allows guests to journey through Pandora's lush forest, encountering the Na'vi culture of Pandora and its wildlife. The ride system is the same as in "Avatar Flight of Passage," with the exception that it is not propelled by rocket power and is available as a family-friendly boat ride.

The particular culture, native plants, and animals of Pandora inspired the Na'vi theatrical lighting and special effects. The Na'vi spiritual beliefs are embodied in a series of haunting indigenous songs performed by an indigenous Na'vi choir. In this experience, the Na'vi culture comes to life uniquely, which will take your breath away.

Date Opened:

May 27, 2017

Wait Times:

25-60 minutes

Lightning Lane:

Yes

Age Restrictions:

Guests must be at least 44 inches tall to ride. All guests must be at least 10 years old to watch the Na'vi River Journey light show and 15 years old to watch the Na'Vi show in The Backstage Studio Theater, which may include mature themes, violence, and loud noises.

Health Restriction:

Guests must be in good health and free from high blood pressure, heart, back, or neck problems, or other conditions that this adventure could aggravate. Expectant mothers should not ride.

Did You Know:

The name "Avatar Flight of Passage" has a double meaning: "flight of passage" represents the feeling of awe one experiences when flying through Pandora's jungle; "avatar" refers to the blue Na'vi warriors that greet you at the end of the attraction. They consider you an avatar for having survived your journey through Pandora's dense jungle and its dangerous inhabitants.

Kilimanjaro Safaris

Image: HarshLight from San Jose

At the loading area, you will board safari trucks that will whisk you away to the start of your African safari. The tour traverses a 100-acre savannah as the tour guide points out some of the 34 species of birds and animals found in the game preserve. On the dashboard of each row of the vehicle are labeled photographs of the passengers. There are antelopes, black rhinos, white rhinos, warthogs, ostriches, giraffes, zebras, elephants, crocodiles, hippos, baboons, white-bearded wildebeests, and lions among these animals.

During the ride, a safari guide educates the audience about some of the wildlife and history of the area, explaining that animals that have been successfully bred in captivity are released into an animal preserve with others of their kind. The savanna is very similar to that of the African Serengeti, with over 15,000 animals living in one place. The savanna allows for natural predator-prey relationships as well as testing both hunting skills and reproduction cycles.

Guests will be able to see unusual and exotic animals that can only be found in South Africa, such as giraffes, elephants, and hippos. On the way back to the "main safari vehicle," you will get off at the leap-frog stop, where you will be pushed backboard into another vehicle in order to view the remainder of the park.

Date Opened:

April 22, 1998

Wait Times:

15 minutes - 2 hours and 30 minutes.

Lightning Lane:

Yes

Age Restrictions:

Guests must be at least 9 years old to ride, but children under age 4 should sit on a parent's lap in the vehicles. All guests must be at least 4'9" tall to ride.

Health Restriction:

Guests must be in good health and free from high blood pressure, heart, back, or neck problems, or other conditions that this adventure could aggravate. Guests with recent injuries, respiratory infections, or those who have a fear of heights should ask to sit on the ground level of the vehicles.

Did You Know:

Kilimanjaro Safaris derives its name from a local term meaning "the stone house," as the park was constructed on the site of a former home.

Festival of the Lion King

Image: Sam Howzit

Festival of the Lion King is a popular live show at Disney's Animal Kingdom that features a virtual explosion of colors, music, and astounding talent. This celebration will feature thirty minutes of a variety of Disney's finest entertainment. You will hear some of the most popular songs from The Lion King performed by magnificent singers. The costumes of the singer and dancers feature an explosion of color, feathers, beads, fringe, and exquisite headdresses. Talented stilt walkers dance with apparent ease to the pounding beat. On enormous moving stages, audio-animatronic and live-costumed characters are introduced. The spectacular conclusion includes a rendition of "Circle of Life" that stirs the heart. It is a feel-good celebration of life and Disney's The Lion King.

Date Opened:

April 22, 1998

Lightning Lane:

Yes

Age Restrictions:

Guests must be at least 7 years old to attend the live show with a parent or guardian.

Health Restriction:

There is no height or weight restriction.

Did You Know:

The "Festival of the Lion King" was inspired by the elaborate ceremonies and colorful costumes of the Zulu tribe of Africa. During these ceremonies, a huge circle is formed by a group of men who sing and dance while they encircle their king. All the while, they chant in time to the beat of their drums and hand-made instruments played by other performers on stilts.

It's Tough to be a Bug

The Tree of Life's It's Tough to Be a Bug! Attraction challenges visitors to experience an insect's life through 3-D and special effects. As part of the attraction, guests will encounter different insects, such as fireflies, walking sticks, and beetles. They are then invited to crawl through a tarantula's cave and other creepy places by moving walkways.

Guests will discover how insects detect their surroundings. They will even learn about some bugs' abilities to spray toxins or emit foul smells as protection from predators. Guests will learn how insects help plants grow, find and defend their homes, and communicate with each other.

Guests will also see how insects are important to the ecosystem. They will see a bug's life cycle and its relationship to the plants they feed upon. They will also discover how they can be beneficial in controlling pests, such as spiders, which can otherwise eat our crops or damaged homes.

Date Opened:

April 22, 1998

Lightning Lane:

Yes

Age Restrictions:

A warning to parents, some of the special effects may be too intense for small children. It may be best for an adult to experience this before bringing small children in to see it.

Health Restriction:

All guests are welcome. There are no height or weight restrictions.

Did You Know:

There will be some moth and spider bites in this section of the attraction, so it is best to wear long pants or cover exposed legs with long pants or shirt sleeves.

Epcot

Soarin' Around the World

Image: Jeremy Thompson from Los Angeles

Each has three rows of seating, with the most desirable being the front row, closest to the screen. When the ride begins, the front row winds up being the highest in the air, and none of the other rows are visible as they go below and slightly to the rear of the row in front.

Although the system looks like a traditional sit-down roller coaster, it uses a free-falling motion. The film begins with an aerial view of land and water worldwide, followed by a smooth vertical drop at 70 mph (112 km/h). As the drop continues, large curved sections are shown. This gives riders a feeling of weightlessness. Then the "hang gliders" fly over various landmarks and cities, such as Venice and Machu Picchu in South America. The birds that appear soar above eagles and other birds flying high up in the cloud layer. They then glide over mountains with clouds below them, causing the audience to feel as if they are flying through the air. Lastly, they fly over various cities around the world, such as Prague and Sydney. Guests can enjoy a view of downtown Los Angeles, Disneyland Resort, and Walt Disney World Resort. During this sequence, you also feel that you are flying in the sky with birds.

Date Opened:

February 8, 2001, film updated June 17, 2016

Wait Time:

Typically 20 to 60 minutes

Ride Length:

4 minutes, 51 seconds

Lightning Lane:

Yes, but first-row seating is limited

Age Restrictions:

Ages 6 and over can ride. Guests must be at least 40 inches (102 cm) tall to ride. A parent or guardian must accompany minors.

Health Restriction:

Pregnant guests with heart, back, or neck problems must take caution while riding.

Did You Know:

Soarin' Around the World was created as a joint project between Disney Imagineering and Lucasfilm Animation.

Image: Michael Gray from Wantagh NY

Guests will design their own custom concept vehicle at an interactive design kiosk so that they will choose all your car's features. Guests will ride through the attraction in a six-passenger SimCar, but your design follows you through the ride in a virtual sense. In the end, you will find out how your design compares to the SimCar in the areas of Capability, Efficiency, Responsiveness, and Power. The soundtrack features not only music but special sound effects as well. There are four show scenes. In Capability, your car is tested for rough roads and weather conditions. Efficiency tests what effect your car will have on the earth. Responsiveness tests the car's maneuverability. Everyone's favorite section is the final one: Speed! As you race around the outside track, you will feel the wind in your hair.

In the post-show, your car will be scored against cars from the rest of the day. Multiple interactive elements allow you to tweak your design to your liking further.

Date Opened:

March 17, 1999(original), December 6, 2012 (reopening),

Waiting Time:

Typically 15 minutes (when not busy)

Ride Length:

4 minutes

Lightning Lane:

Yes

Age Restrictions:

For participation, riders must be at least 6 years old. Guests within any age group must be accompanied by a supervising adult aged 21 or older.

Health Restriction:

Guests may experience strong vibrations, sudden movements, and rapid changes in direction throughout the attraction. Back or neck injuries may be aggravated by this attraction. Pregnant guests should not ride. Any persons who have heart or back conditions, motion sickness, or similar physical conditions that this attraction could aggravate are not permitted to ride without assistance from a responsible companion.

Did You Know:

Test Track has the world's most comprehensive set of advanced automotive design tools and the most advanced 3D projection system on planet Earth.

Frozen Ever After

Frozen Ever After is a musical ride in Epcot at the Walt Disney World Resort that reverses Shoot the Chute. The attraction in the Norway Pavilion of Epcot's World Showcase features scenes inspired by Disney's animated film Frozen and the 2015 animated short Frozen Fever. The ride takes place in Arendelle, the kingdom of Arendelle, located in the arctic region of Norway, where Kristoff and Anna have a royal wedding. The attraction uses a track system which makes it similar to a roller coaster. At the end of each ride, guests are brought back into Tomorrowland, from which they departed on the ride.

Date Opened:

June 21, 2016

Ride Length:

15 minutes

Lightning Lane:

Yes

Age Restrictions:

Ages 3 and up can ride. A parent or guardian must accompany minors.

Health Restriction:

Guests should expect to encounter a combination of intense effects, including fog, strobe lights, sudden actions, bright colors, and swirling effects. Guests may experience strong vibrations.

Did You Know:

The attraction features Audio-Animatronics figures and projections of characters from the film. The attraction's new state-of-the-art ride system is inspired by Disney's classic boat rides that travel through Norway's beautiful fjords.

Spaceship Earth

Image:chensiyuan

The attraction is a slow-moving dark ride with a slow ascent up to the top of the sphere; then, it travels around the inside of the sphere while low-energy lights illuminate scenes from notable historical events. The attraction uses a ride system similar to the one used in Great Moments with Mr. Lincoln.

Date Opened:

June 6, 1982 (original) March 16, 1994 (reopening)

Waiting Time:

Typically 30 minutes

Ride Length:

3 minutes, 39 seconds (original), 4 minutes (reopening)

Ride Length:

8 minutes 20 seconds with no pre-show or post-show

1 hour 30 minutes with pre-show and post-show

Lightning Lane:

Yes

Age Restrictions:

Ages 10 and up can ride. A parent or guardian must accompany minors.

Health Restriction:

This attraction is a constant low-speed dark ride with no sudden movements. Pregnant women are allowed to experience the attraction, but it may not be comfortable for them as the ride is bumpy due to the slow ascent of Spaceship Earth. Guests with back problems should also avoid going to this attraction. Guests should NOT ride on this attraction if they have any of the following conditions:

- Neck, back, or heart problems

- Motion sickness

- Sensitivity to strobe lights, glare, loud noises, or similar conditions

Did You Know:

This is the tallest attraction in the World Showcase. For a tour of Spaceship Earth, guests can meet with an audio/visual guide who will show them the inner workings of this attraction.

Photo By: Christopher H (Tripadvisor)

This unique performance, Drawn to Life, was developed in partnership with Cirque du Soleil, Walt Disney Animation Studios, and Walt Disney Imagineering. It pays homage to the exceptional craftsmanship of Disney by celebrating the art of Disney animation in Cirque du Soleil's signature style. New, original acrobatic sequences, dazzling choreography, musical masterworks, and whimsical characters will transport the audience into the world of Disney animation.

Ticket Prices:

Ages 10 and up - from $99 to $169, depending on the seats you want to see the show.

Ages 3 - 9 - from $79 to $135, depending on the seats you want to see the show.

Ages 2 - below - Free

Did You Know:

Written and directed by Michel Laprise, with Fabrice Becker serving as Director of Creation, Drawn to Life is a live acrobatic journey that tells the story of Julie, a determined girl who discovers an unexpected gift left by her Disney animator father: an unfinished animation.

Image: Scottb211

This upscale, family-friendly bowling alley elevates this traditional pastime with its contemporary décor, haute cuisine, live music, dancing, and billiards. There are 30 bowling lanes at Splitsville. A lane concierge will deliver your shoes and assist you in setting up your game. When you arrive, everyone's names will be displayed on a screen above the field, and scoring will be performed automatically. Typically, bowling is first come, first served. A few days in advance, lanes can be reserved for large groups.

Bowling Prices:

Weekdays:

Day Time (10 a.m. to 4 a.m.) - $17

Evening (4 p.m. to close) - $22

Weekends:

All Day & Evenings (open to close) - $22 per person

Bowling Time:

The bowling time depends on the size of your party. Instead of paying by the hour, you pay per person.

- 1-2 People: 1 Hour

- 3-4 People: 1 Hour 15 Minutes

- 5-6 People: 1 Hour 30 Minutes

- 7-8 People: 1 Hour 45 Minutes

Priority Bowling:

Splitsville offers Priority Bowling for groups of eight or fewer. This will get you into the fast lane. Priority Bowling entitles your group to the next available lane upon check-in, subject to any other Priority Bowling party or lane reservation.

Weekdays:

Day Time (10 a.m. to 4 a.m.) - $27

Evening (4 p.m. to close) - $32

Weekends:

All Day & Evenings (open to close) - $32 per person

Early Bird Bowling

Splitsville also offers an Early Bird Bowling special that is available every day from open until 12 p.m. Pricing is a little cheaper during the Early Bird Special. This offer is not available on select holidays and other blackout dates.

- Kids (9 & Under) – $10

- Adults - $14

Splitsville is great for those who are looking to have a little fun with their family and friends. It is a great place to go on a date or have fun with the family. Stay after bowling, and enjoy the atmosphere of Splitsville.

There are other attractions available at Disney World; do not limit yourself to the one listed here.

Over the next few months, Walt Disney World will see a lot of new things. The completion and return of two highly anticipated projects are anticipated for 2023. Additionally, a few of the projects originally scheduled for 2022 will be completed in 2023.

The following projects are expected to open in 2023:

Disney's EPCOT Transformation

EPCOT has undergone a multi-year transformation over the past few years that is anticipated to be finished by the end of the year. There has been a lot going on for EPCOT visitors over the past few years. Guests have witnessed the emergence of new EPCOT attractions, buildings, entertainment, and neighborhoods, to name a few, as a result of a massive transformation that has ushered EPCOT into a new era.

World of Nature will debut Journey of Water this fall, Inspired by Moana. This self-guided trail leads visitors through the natural water cycle. This goes from the skies to the oceans and then back to the beginning. Guests will be encouraged to become defenders and allies of natural resources, just as Moana did.

Additionally, CommuniCore Hall will open later this year. World Celebration will be the focal point of EPCOT's festival programming when it opens. According to new Disney illustrations, this will also be the location of a new character greeting location known as Mickey & Friends. This colorful location will be where guests can meet Mickey Mouse and his pals.

Additionally, CommuniCore Hall will feature a dynamic exhibition space. It will be altered for the arrival of each EPCOT festival throughout the year. Artwork depicting what the EPCOT International Festival of the Arts could look like has been released. This manipulates the space's lights, shapes, and reflections. Walt Disney Imagineering designed the structure to honor the legacy of EPCOT and the original CommuniCore buildings.

This year, the next EPCOT project to be completed is the transformation of Future World. This is anticipated to be completed by the end of summer. A Care and Share center will be located in Innoventions West at Epcot. It will serve as a resource for visitors. Disney provided the Disney Parks Blog with new concept art depicting how it may appear when it opens later this spring.

Image: M Town Citizen

Location:

Magic Kingdom

Opens:

April 4, 2023

Tron Lightcycle Power Run, a brand-new coaster-style attraction coming to Magic Kingdom, was inspired by a similar ride at Shanghai Disneyland. Originally intended to be a part of the 50th anniversary of Walt Disney World. This incredible new roller coaster will place riders on a two-wheeled "lightning cycle" before sending them on an exhilarating journey to the digital frontier. The attraction will feature a number of high-flying elements, including a new loop known as the Mad Miles Loop, along with multiple other inversions and thrilling twists. Along the way, guests will be entertained by guest interaction opportunities with scenes from the hit movie TRON: Legacy.

While this new attraction will open during the International Festival of the Arts later this month, it is expected to begin its operation several months after that. This is to allow phase one of the TRON Lightcycle Power Run (lasting approximately one year) to be completed. When its second phase begins, they are expected to add additional elements and variations based on fan feedback gathered during the construction and testing phases for the attraction.

Disney World is scheduled to have a number of new attractions, venues, and experiences open in the next few years. These projects are just the beginning of Disney World's journey through the next decade. With that in mind, it's important for guests to keep in mind that opening dates aren't always guaranteed. Always be sure to check the Disney World website for more information regarding opening dates before planning your next trip.

CONCLUSION

The Walt Disney World Resort is one of the most fun destinations in the world; it is a place where memories are made. There are countless attractions, activities, exceptional dining options, and nighttime entertainment venues that you can enjoy with your family, friends, or someone special. This guide helps you plan your vacation accordingly and ensure you don't miss any of the exciting attractions, amazing views, and delicious food!

You should have the time of your life at Walt Disney World, as there are so many things to do and see, but only if you conduct extensive research beforehand. You need to know your priorities and how to manage your time most effectively.

Managing your way through Epcot or anywhere in the Magic Kingdom may seem simple; however, the last thing you want to have is a lagging crowd and no family time. The best way to ensure there is plenty of time for everything is to first make a list of all your priorities and things that you want to see most – put them in order of priority, allocate budget and timeframe accordingly, and plan accordingly. It's easy! All you have to do is plan, plan, and plan!

Enjoy your vacation, have fun, and enjoy yourself!

SCAN ME

Download and Print Your Packing List!

Printed in Great Britain
by Amazon

20571922R00081